30 Days ot Whole Food

120 Irresistible and Healthy Recipes

A 30 Day Whole Food Challenge That Will Help You Lose Weight, Boost Your Metabolism, and Prevent Disease

Table of Contents

Chapter 10 - Dinner

Chapter 11 - Condiments + Dressings

I would love to give you a bonus. Please visit happyhealthycookingonline.com and get these 4 amazing eBooks for FREE!

Introduction

What exactly are "whole foods?" Why are they so good for you? Many years ago, every food was a whole food. We ate fresh vegetables, fruit, nuts, and meat that were free from artificial processing, chemicals, and preservatives. However, all that changed when food companies realized they could make more money by selling food originally manufactured for the military to society at large. They began making food last longer, grow bigger, and taste "better." To accomplish these goals, food was stripped of important nutrients and bulked up with synthetic ingredients. After years of living on such a diet, for most people the consequences are clear: heart disease, obesity, digestion problems, and more.

Luckily, you can get back to basics and begin a whole-food diet today! This book provides you with shopping help, diet tips, and 120 recipes, so the next 30 days on whole foods will be as rewarding as possible. After 30 days, you'll get a good idea of what whole foods can do for your health, including improved digestion, higher energy levels, and less cravings for processed food.

This isn't a *diet* in the traditional sense. It isn't about tough restrictions or feeling hungry all the time. Instead, you'll feel happy, cleansed, and amazed at what small changes can do for your body. That's what the whole-foods diet is all about - feeling *whole*.

Chapter 1 - What's the Deal with Whole Foods?

So, what is a "whole food" anyway? It's a term that's thrown around a lot, but what foods are actually "whole?" Whole foods are basically any food item in its natural state, which means it hasn't been processed or refined, and it hasn't had fat, sugar, or salt added to it. This includes fresh vegetable and fruit produce, beans that don't come in a can, and organic meats. Basically, if you look at the nutritional info on a product, and it has a long list of ingredients you can't pronounce, in all likelihood, it is not a whole food.

> Eating Tip
>
> As an example, for beef jerky, you want the label to read something like: "100% grass-fed beef," "water," "salt," "black pepper" and "garlic powder." As a general rule, you want to stick to making your own food from bare-bones ingredients: beef + dehydrator + seasonings = homemade beef jerky.

The foundation of the whole-foods lifestyle is threefold: carbs, fat, and protein. Your carbs should be healthy carbs and come from whole grains, instead of ones that have been refined or otherwise stripped down. Keep in mind that "whole-wheat" does not mean "whole-grain." Your protein should come from sources (almost always organic meats, beans, and legumes) rich in very specific amino acids that help balance and maintain your metabolism. Fat, which is almost always the bad guy in every other diet, is crucial for your organs and tissue to heal themselves and stay strong. Good fat also protects against memory loss, joint pain, and symptoms of mental illnesses like depression and ADHD. You do have to be careful about what kind of fat you're eating and where it comes from however. Healthy fats include Omega-3 fatty acids and monounsaturated fatty acids. We'll get into what specific carbs, fats, and proteins to eat in a later chapter.

While the phrase "whole foods" has been flying around a lot recently, whole foods are nothing new. Every kind of food used to be "whole," it's only been in the last century that humans have started pumping food full of artificial preservatives, flavors, colors, and so on, which you'll learn about in the next chapter. The roots of the whole-food movement can be traced back to scientific researchers, writers, and nature-lovers who caught on to the idea of "organic" food. In the 1920's through the 1940's, these pioneers began to write about how everything is connected - soil, plants, livestock, and people. Before then, all farming had been organic, and there hadn't been a reason to feel passionate about it. The early organic advocates were really just talking about the past and the "old ways" of doing things. Instead of trying to drastically manipulate plants and animals, like killing crop pests with nerve gas, their belief was that it was more effective and ultimately healthier to work *with* nature instead of in opposition to it.

One of these writers, Sir Albert Howard, composed a famous organic farming book in 1940 called "An Agricultural Testament." He addressed how new changes to agriculture (most significantly, chemical fertilizers) were unwise, and that methods like composting were better. He also drew a link between human health and agricultural methods, saying that "the whole problem in health in soil, plant, animal, and man [should be grouped] as one great subject."

In 1946, influenced by Howard, a Quaker named F. Newman Turner began practicing organic gardening on a 200-acre farm and set up the Whole Food Society where organic farmers could connect with customers seeking organic produce. Turner coined the term "whole foods" in his magazine, "The Farmer," which earned a small but committed readership worldwide. Turner's farm, Goosegreen Farm, soon became a hotspot for people interested in growing natural food.

Turner eventually sold the Goosegreen Farm and began to study human and animal health. In the 1950's until his death, he worked as a supplier for natural pet foods and herbal medicines, and founded a company that imported herbal remedies and health food from Europe.

In 1980, Whole Foods opened with the vision to provide all-natural foods to the public. The 1970's and '80's was a time when interest in organic food was spreading. Years of research finally started to expose just how dangerous chemicals and food processing was, and consumers were ready for good old-fashioned whole foods. The Whole Foods company has faced significant criticism over how it labels its food in addition to its high prices, so I cannot endorse them as the one-stop-shop for everything organic and whole. I'll get into where you can buy whole foods in the chapter on shopping.

The whole-food movement is about rejecting processed and going back to basics. Other terms you might have heard that are similar to whole foods include farm-to-table, which places an emphasis on local food sources, and "clean eating," which is extremely similar to a whole-foods diet, but unlike with clean eating, a whole-foods diet allows you to eat whole-milk dairy products.

People like Howard and Turner took on the crusade for real food as a response to more "innovative" ways of farming, and the more recent push for whole foods is also a response to how the food industry is changing. The next chapters will dig deeper into the specifics and history of processed foods and GMOs.

Chapter 2 - When and Why Did Food Become so Processed?

A 1911 ad

Crisco—Better than butter for cooking

What exactly are we dealing with when we talk about processed foods vs. whole foods? How and when did food become such a major factor in our country's increasingly bad health? While we think of processed foods as being very recent, they actually date back to the 1890's with the creation of trans fats. Industrial factories created artificial trans fats by adding hydrogen to vegetable oils to make foods like margarine more spreadable and convenient for fast use. Procter & Gamble was the first major company to release a hydrogenated product, Crisco, in 1911. Other processed foods at this time included Oreos, Hellmann's mayonnaise, Nathan's hot dogs, and Aunt Jemima syrup.

By the 1920's, food companies wanted to appeal to women who didn't want to spend so much time cooking. This required more additives that would preserve food longer, and frozen foods. Brands like Wonder Bread, Velveeta, VanCamp's, Welch's and Peter Pan peanut butter became popular. In 1937, Kraft burst on the scene with its macaroni-and-cheese, which could last for 10 months without refrigeration, and was cheap enough for everyone dealing with war rations. After WWII ended, a lot of the foods created for soldiers, like instant coffee and cake mix, were integrated into mainstream culture.

M&M's and Cheetos also entered stores during the 1940's, and the first McDonald's and Dairy Queen opened their doors, beginning America's love affair with fast food. On the farms, fertilization and irrigation took off, which leeched nutrients from plants. The corn and soy lobbies became more aggressive, and the government started providing subsidies, making it financially-advantageous for more food companies to produce high fructose corn syrup, modified corn starches, and trans fats.

Processed food reached its peak in the 1950's. The new microwave was a big hit, new highways allowed for the success of fast food restaurants and mass food distribution, and foods like Swanson TV dinners, Sweet 'n Low, and Cheez Whiz hit the shelves.

The next few decades weren't much better. Though people started to figure out that all this high-fat, high-calorie food might not be great for them, the solution was just more packaged vegetables, "diet" and "health" drinks like Gatorade and Crystal Light, and sugar substitutes like aspartame. Society was fooled into believing that low-calorie equals healthy, so all food companies had to do was remove oils and butter from food like dairy products, and pack them with artificial, zero-calorie ingredients to maintain taste.

In the 1990's, we finally get some good news. Food companies became required by law to include nutritional labels, and studies started to reveal the health consequences of artificial, processed food. While the full effect of processed foods on humans is not fully-known, we do know that food becomes much less nutritious when it's exposed to all kinds of chemicals and additives. For one, processed foods often have hydrogenated oils, which are shown to clog up people's arteries. They are also packed with sugar - even store-bought is packed with it, leading to food addictions and high carbs. Processed foods also tend to have less fiber while still containing a high amount of calories, which leads to overeating, because you don't feel full without fiber.

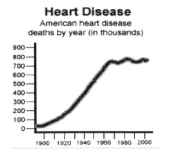

Heart Disease
American heart disease
deaths by year (in thousands)

Source: http://www.commercecreators.
com/sites/folder1394/site_images_system/user/heartcha
rt.jpg

It isn't hard to see what exactly was (and still is) happening to people. With the way processed foods are created, they are so full of fat and sugar that they become literally addictive, leading to widespread overeating. Since processed food was introduced, heart disease and obesity rates have gone up, while many artificial ingredients (Sodium Nitrates and Sodium Nitrites, artificial colors, BHA) have been linked to cancer despite being labeled as "safe" by the FDA. One of the most famous examples of processed foods gone bad was Alar (official name Daminozide), which was a growth regulator used to delay the ripening process for apples. In 1989, a 60 Minute special revealed that this synthetic was dangerous for humans, especially children. People freaked out and the agricultural industry lost $100 million dollars. It all ended when the EPA banned the use of Alar in crops.

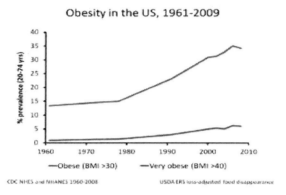

Obesity in the US, 1961-2009

In addition to all the artificial ingredients that have been connected to serious health problems, a newer food trend to be aware of when considering a whole-food diet is the rise of GMOs. The next chapter will get into what exactly a GMO is, how they have evolved throughout history, and why you should avoid them.

Chapter 3- What are GMOs?

GMOS (genetically-modified organisms) are any type of plant or animal that has had its DNA manipulated through genetic engineering. The most common GMOs right now are agricultural crops like soy, corn, and cotton. While there's been a lot of fuss about GMOs recently, they've actually been around in some form for thousands of years.

In prehistoric times, people were able to strengthen their plants and animals through selective breeding, which makes sense. Of course early humans would choose the best of the best - the literal cream of the crop - to improve their crops and livestock. Over the millenias, crops radically changed and would have never existed in the wild if it hadn't been for humans. Think wheat, corn, strawberries, and so on - if humans hadn't been messing with them, these crops wouldn't exist. However, they were using natural methods, which is why the food they produced would still be considered whole food. It's when you bring in synthetics and gene splicing that things get a little more complicated.

Modern GMOs as we know them originate with a company called Monsanto. They began in the early 1900's as a producer of saccharin and vanillin, sweet food additives, and then eventually turned to industrial chemicals in the 1920's. Their products included sulfuric acid and PCBs, and then plastics like synthetic fibers. Other significant creations include the pesticide DDT and the infamous Agent Orange.

DDT ended up being banned in 1972 after its introduction in 1939. Research revealed that DDT builds up in the human system, and causes incredible harm to birds. The chlorinated hydrocarbons pesticide weakens eggshells, resulting in a decreased number of birds like the bald eagle. Rachel Carson (was one of the pioneering writers I mentioned earlier), wrote *Silent Spring* as a direct reference to all the birds killed by DDT.

Agent Orange was a herbicide used in the Vietnam War to remove the thick jungle cover. Over 4.8 million Vietnamese civilians were exposed and poisoned. At least 400,000 died and millions suffered from cancer, skin diseases, and birth defects. The toxin can still be found through genetic illnesses and contaminated soil. Monsanto eventually had to pay out $180 million to Vietnam veterans who were exposed, but zilch to the Vietnamese. After DDT was banned, Monsanto developed the weed-killer glyphosate (commercially-known as Roundup), in 1974.

This is a pretty frightening origin story considering how Monsanto seems to be in the business of destroying life, not creating it. How did the company make this odd shift to growing crops? In 1972 to 1973, two biochemists figured out how to "cut and paste" pieces of DNA into other organisms. Three years later, this biotechnology went commercial, allowing companies like Monsanto to begin playing with the genetic makeup of food. In 1983, Monsanto's first genetically-modified plants were created, and in 1988, they tried out their first soybean crop. Soybeans would soon become the most common GMO, and they were manipulated to be resistant to glyphosate, the very pesticide that Monsanto had created.

Other crops have since popped up from Monsanto and other companies like DuPont. Cotton, sugar beets, tomatoes, and rice have been genetically-engineered to hold up against pesticides, as well as insects and other disease. Monsanto didn't stick to plant food though; in 1994, they released rBGH and rBST, bovine growth hormones that made cows produce more milk. These hormones have been linked to breast and prostate cancer, to name just a few.

In 2013, 80% of the US' corn sprouted from Monsanto GMO seeds, while 93% of soy also came from Monsanto. However, you won't be able to tell what foods came from GMOs. In July of 2015, the House passed a bill that prevented states from requiring GMO labeling of any food products. Essentially, this means the food industry is allowed to keep consumers in the dark about what is and isn't a GMO. Their argument is that labeling something a GMO will make people believe there is something wrong with GMOS, when, according to companies like Monsanto, GMOs are "perfectly safe." The problem with that is that there is no way for Monsanto to know if GMOs are actually totally safe. There just hasn't been enough time and research to discover what the long term effects might be. As you read before, lots of things were once labeled "safe," but eventually turned out to be contributing to increased risk of cancer and other illnesses. Here are some other reasons to avoid GMOs:

- They hurt the environment
  The increased use of herbicides with GMO crops (because the crops are resistant) results in more harm to birds, amphibians, marine life, and other creatures.

- Research that criticizes GMOs are suppressed
  It's automatically suspicious that anti-GMO research and advocates are so frequently censored.

- Monsanto's other creations were once considered "safe"
  Monsanto's track record is not great when it comes to human and environmental health. We should definitely not drop on the GMO train until we know a bit more about the effects.

Even if GMOs do turn out to be totally safe, what's the harm in letting people know what they're eating? While it is possible that the bill won't pass Congress or might be vetoed by the president, it seems likely that the incredibly powerful and wealthy food companies will get their way.

In response, lots of grocery stores are taking action and labeling food themselves. However, you should know there is a difference between something labeled "non-GMO" versus "organic." Non-GMO literally just means they aren't GMO - it *doesn't* mean that synthetic pesticides, herbicides, or even antibiotics shown to lead to antibiotic resistance were not used. If you really want good, whole food, go with organic every time.

So, you know why processed foods and GMOs can be bad for y our health, so why
are whole foods good?

Chapter 4 - Why Whole Foods Are so Good

You know why processed and refined foods are so bad, but why are whole foods so good? To find out, we need to break whole foods down to their skeletons and take a look at the minerals and vitamins inside them.

Phytochemicals

These little guys are also called phytonutrients, and there are hundreds of them living in plants.

A few of these phytochemicals include anthocyanins, which are in dark berries; lycopene, which is an antioxidant and present in tomatoes; pterostilbene, which makes cells break down cholesterol and fat.

People like to buy supplements that are supposedly rich in a particular phytochemical, but there is no proof that this actually does anything. It appears that a lot of the nutritional value may be in how all these phytochemicals interact with each other within whole foods.

B6 and B12

B vitamins can be found in lots of whole foods, with B6 popping up in whole grains, beans, nuts, chicken, fish, and B12 in beef, eggs, fish, and dairy. These vitamins are essential for a healthy circulatory and immune system. There is no reason to take a supplement, unless you're a vegan, because B12 is only found in animal products.

Vitamin C

Ah, good ol' vitamin C. Most people point to citrus fruits as the best sources of vitamin C, but that honor actually belongs to greens like broccoli, spinach, kale, and Brussels sprouts. Of course, vitamin C is also present in oranges and strawberries, and all you need to get your daily requirement is to eat one orange. Vitamin C is an antioxidant that maintains your immune system and the "good" cholesterol, HDL.

Vitamin D

Vitamin D is a necessary vitamin because it allows your body to absorb calcium. Your body actually produces its own vitamin D when you're out and about in the sunshine, but you need to get most of the vitamin D from food, especially if you can't be in the sun that often. Drink milk, eat salmon, and enjoy a bowl of whole-grain cereal.

Vitamin E

Another antioxidant, vitamin E is especially good for eye health and might be able to stop Alzheimer's disease. The main sources of E come from veggie oils like olive and canola, seeds, and avocados. Vitamin E is a fat-soluble vitamin, which means it is possible to have "too much" in your system, so don't go overboard with the avocado or seeds. These foods are typically high in fat anyway (good fat, but still a lot of it), so it is easy to stay within safe limits.

Fiber

Fiber is essential for healthy and regular bowel movements, and is found in whole plants. It is also great because it makes you feel fuller, so you are less likely to overeat when you have fiber-rich foods like raspberries, lentils, broccoli, green peas, and barley.

Folic acid

Folic acid comes up the most during a woman's pregnancy, because not eating enough of this can cause risks for birth defects. However, if anyone has low folic acid, they become at risk for cancer and heart disease. Get your folic acid from dark leafy greens like broccoli, and also whole grains and beans.

Iron

To prevent anemia, you got to get your iron. Good iron levels have also been connected to healthy immune systems and better memory. The best food source for iron is found in red meat, though you can also get some from chicken, fish, and legumes. If you don't eat meat, you'll probably have to take an iron supplement.

Zinc

This is another mineral that is found in animals products (beef, pork, oysters), though you can also get zinc from cashews, pumpkin seeds, and chickpeas. Zinc is also the only proven way to shorten and weaken the common cold, unlike products like Airborne.

Those are all the "sciency" reasons why whole foods are good for you, but what does that all mean, exactly? How will eating whole foods make you feel? There are lots of benefits to getting all the nutrients above (and then some) from whole foods.

1. You'll have better digestion

    Countless people have a troublesome relationship with food because it messes up their stomachs. This is most likely because they aren't getting enough fiber. When you eat whole foods like vegetables, fruit, nuts, and whole grains, your body is able to process everything properly. You'll be regular, less bloated, and just all-around more comfortable in your body.

2. Your blood sugar will even out

    If you don't have diabetes, you might not even know how much a rollercoaster-blood sugar system is affecting your life. When your blood sugar is low, you feel tired and grumpy. The usual solution is to eat something too high in sugary carbs, which causes an upward swing and then another crash. When you're eating whole foods like fresh veggies as a snack instead of sugary yogurt or an energy drink, your blood sugar will stay even for longer instead of crashing so you won't need to eat again immediately.

3. You'll feel younger and more energetic

    Your body has to work really hard to break down processed foods and wring out the small amount of nutrients still left. After all that work, it's no wonder you're always feeling tired and unmotivated. By ditching processed foods and choosing whole foods, which your body was designed to love, life won't seem quite so hard anymore. You'll have more energy at work and to do other things that you've been exhausted to tackle, like more exercise or new hobbies.

4. Your weight will be easier to manage

    Processed foods are packed with high calories, bad carbs, and bad fats that lead to weight gain. They also contain very little fiber, which means even though you just ate, you're going to be hungry again very soon. When you eat whole foods, you are not only snacking on foods that are lower in calories, but they are full of the fiber that makes you satisfied for longer. Managing your weight and losing weight will become much easier than if you were relying on processed, packaged foods for your diet. Also, the longer you stick to the whole foods diet, the less you will crave your old vices, so managing your weight will be easier long-term.

5. You lower your risk for disease

    With the way Americans eat, it's not surprising how many of us get heart disease and diabetes. All the red meat and saturated fats clog up our arteries, and a high consumption of sugar leads to insulin resistance, which leads to type 2 diabetes. However, when you are on a whole-foods diet, the high amount of fiber you consume will significantly lower your risk for heart disease, and the even blood sugar levels that whole foods generates keeps diabetes at bay. Also, all the phytochemicals and additional nutrients have been shown to play a part in preventing other diseases, like cancers and Alzheimer's. If you are at a genetic risk for a disease, it is especially important to go on a whole-foods diet to protect yourself.

There's really no "dark side" to eating whole foods, health-wise. Hopefully you're at least curious about changing your diet. The next chapter will teach you how to shop for whole foods and give you a specific list of the "yes" foods and "no" foods. When you see how easy (and affordable) it really can be, you'll definitely want to make the change!

Chapter 5- How to Shop on a Whole-Foods Diet

Now that you know a bit about the whole-foods diet, you'll want to restock your pantry and get rid of the processed junk. This can be a tough part of the process - there's the store, all laid out in front of you, and you have no idea what to get. Keep in mind, you don't *have* to go to Whole Foods, despite the name. While the Whole Foods store does pride itself on its selection, it doesn't come cheap. You can get whole foods anywhere, and don't let anyone tell you that you have to spend a fortune. The reality is that eating a whole-foods diet ends up being cheaper than depending on packaged, processed foods. The compromise is time, because preparing whole-food meals does take longer than throwing something in the oven or microwave. Just take a look back at the benefits of whole-foods if you're feeling wary.

Before you even get to the store, it's best to write a list. That way, you can stay focused on what you really need (instead of being tempted by processed junk) and you'll know for sure that what you're getting fits into the whole-foods category. Put a variety of whole foods on your list - it's good to try a bunch of stuff and find out what you really like.

Once you're at the store, start getting really good at looking at labels. A good rule of thumb is that no product you buy should have more than, say, 5 ingredients, and they should all be real ingredients. Let's break down what is allowed on a whole-foods diet and what you'll have to say no to. There will be overlap, because many foods serve as sources of carbs, protein, *and* fat.

<u>Good carbs to buy</u>

- ☑ Dark, leafy greens
- ☑ Onions
- ☑ Bell peppers
- ☑ Green beans
- ☑ Eggplant
- ☑ Root vegetables
- ☑ Squash
- ☑ Tomatoes

- ☑ Berries
- ☑ Melons
- ☑ Stone fruits
- ☑ Grapes
- ☑ Brown rice
- ☑ Millet
- ☑ Quinoa
- ☑ Bran
- ☑ Almond/coconut flour

Bad carbs

- ☒ White rice
- ☒ White bread
- ☒ Quick oats
- ☒ Packaged baked goods
- ☒ Boxed breakfast cereal
- ☒ Boxed pasta
- ☒ Pancake mix
- ☒ White flour
- ☒ Wheat flour
- ☒ Frozen pizza

Good proteins to buy

- ☑ Mercury-free, wild-caught fish
- ☑ Tofu
- ☑ Miso
- ☑ Soybeans
- ☑ Free-range, organic lean chicken
- ☑ Grass-fed, organic lean red meats (beef, pork, lamb)
- ☑ Grass-fed, organic 2% or whole milk
- ☑ Plain Greek yogurt w/ no added sugar
- ☑ Nut milk
- ☑ Lentils
- ☑ Chickpeas
- ☑ Dried black beans
- ☑ Dried pinto beans

Bad proteins

- ☒ Honey-roasted/sweetened nuts
- ☒ Canned baked beans

- ☒ Factory-farmed fish
- ☒ Canned fish
- ☒ Processed beef jerky/beef sticks
- ☒ Regular peanut butter
- ☒ Sugary yogurts
- ☒ Hot dogs/brats/breakfast sausages
- ☒ Energy/protein bars
- ☒ Non-organic, processed bacon

Good fats to buy

- ☑ Walnuts
- ☑ Sunflower seeds
- ☑ Pumpkin seeds
- ☑ Raw almonds
- ☑ Raw cashews
- ☑ In-the-shell, unsalted peanuts
- ☑ Pecans
- ☑ Salmon
- ☑ Avocados
- ☑ Whole grains
- ☑ Organic olives
- ☑ Olive oil
- ☑ Cold-pressed, organic coconut oil
- ☑ Grass-fed butter
- ☑ Canola/rapeseed oil
- ☑ Natural peanut butter (check the ingredients label- just peanuts and salt)

Bad fats

- ☒ Vegetable oil
- ☒ French fries
- ☒ Candy
- ☒ Potato chips
- ☒ Fast food
- ☒ Frozen entrees
- ☒ Ice cream
- ☒ Canned soup (especially cream-based ones)
- ☒ Salad dressings

What about the sweet stuff? Depending on if you're following a specific whole-food diet (Whole30 only allows 100% fruit juice as a sweetener), the rules are different, but for this book, you can buy raw honey, 100% organic pure vanilla extract, and 100% pure maple syrup. People are also divisive about chocolate, with some saying it needs to be a minimum of 70% cacao while others say 100%, which is probably a lot more bitter than most people like. We'll say that you can use baking cocoa, but look for words like "100% organic, "raw," "unsweetened," and "unprocessed."

Buying Tip:

Brands like Pure Natural Miracles, Viva Labs, and Freedom Superfoods sell 100% raw cocoa powder.

It's best to just stay away from candy chocolate for the 30 days (with the exception of the 70% organic dark chocolate chunks in the Cherry Chocolate Nice Cream recipe I've included in the "Sweet or Salty Snacks" chapter - it's just too good to leave out!)

Since this book also contains over 100 recipes, feel free to use the ingredient lists as a shopping guide. Personally, I like to base my grocery lists around the meals I've planned for the week - it saves me money because I'm not buying unnecessary ingredients that might spoil, and I know that I'm getting a good variety of tasty, whole foods.

Chapter 6- How to Eat Whole Foods Away from Your Home

It's one thing to stick to a new diet when you're at home. It's another thing entirely when you're out with friends or traveling. You can't possibly just bring your own meals with you everywhere, so how do you stay faithful to whole foods in a new environment, especially an entirely unfamiliar city? Let's break it down into manageable pieces, starting with a night out on the town with friends or family.

At restaurants

When you're just beginning your whole-foods diet, spontaneous dining-out isn't really a good idea. If you have at least a few hours in advance, though, you can pull it off. The first thing you'll want to do is research the restaurant. Do they feature grass-fed beef, and organic fish and chicken? You may have to call them and talk to a manager to find out. Don't worry about being annoying - lots of people have concerns about factory-farmed meat, so your questions shouldn't be unfamiliar to any decent restaurant. If the proteins aren't organic, you can still eat there, but you can make certain choices that are better than others.

- Best - fish
- Acceptable - sirloin steak, other lean cuts of red meat
- Okay - chicken/standard plain hamburger

It's also a good idea to be familiar with the different cooking methods and which are best. The reason this matters is because of the kind of oil used:

- Steamed - really no oil is used, but make sure the other seasonings don't include artificial stuff like MSG
- Grilled - sometimes a little veggie oil is used
- Sautéed - cooked in oil or fat, so confirm the oil is all-natural, like an olive oil
- Roasted - basted in oil so the food doesn't dry out, ask what the oil is
- Fried - lots of processed vegetable oil, do not eat

Once you've picked your protein and chosen a cooking method, it's time to tackle the sides. Most places allow for substitutions or choose-your-own side, so go with simple roasted vegetables or a green salad (no dressing) every time. If it comes with potato, ask to sub a sweet potato in its place. For drinks, you'll have to stick with water with a lemon or lime wedge, since pretty much everything else that's not straight-up soda will still be made with an artificial syrup and tons of sugar.

While traveling

The secret to sticking to whole foods while traveling is *planning*. Before you even leave, lay out a list of all the meals you will be eating while you're away from your home, including snacks. The first meal set to tackle is dinners. This will require quite a bit of research about restaurants in the area. Sites like Yelp and Open Table are very helpful. There are a couple of things you should look for:

- The restaurant takes reservations - this way, you can reserve a table/tables for as long as you are traveling, and don't have to stress about it once you're actually there.
- The place has at least a few options for you - google terms like "grass-fed," "organic," and so on to narrow your restaurant search right away.
- The restaurant is a reasonable distance from your hotel, conference center, etc. - you don't want to have to drive a long way for food

> **Eating Tip:**
> Odds are, you're eating with coworkers, so try to designate yourself as the person who makes the food arrangements. Oftentimes, the boss has at least one place he/she wants to go, so that's out of your control, but you can almost always find something you can eat even if you don't get time in advance to check out the menu.

The next meal is lunch, which is easier in terms of food choices. You will in most cases find salads and other light whole-food fare at any restaurant or even cafeteria, if there's one at the conference/work event you're going to. Write down the lunch-place options in the area, as well as the food options you know are acceptable.

For breakfast and snacks, you should also find a grocery store that's close to your hotel, and make sure your hotel has a fridge. As soon as you reach your destination, head to the store and stock up on whole-food essentials like fruit, veggies, nuts, milk, and yogurt. Some hotels don't serve hot breakfasts (like eggs) along with the usual continental stuff, so you might find yourself faced with a deathtrap of donuts and Danishes. Have a healthy option back at your room, like plain yogurt with some fresh fruit. For a snack, carry around a bag of nuts-and-seeds, fruit like an orange, apple, or banana, and cut celery, carrots, and/or cucumber.

So, once you're all ready to go, you should have done the following:
- Made dinner reservations at whole-food friendly restaurants in the area for every night you're gone
- Made a list of lunch options
- Checked and made sure there's a grocery store near your hotel
- Have a plan for snacks and breakfast using grocery-bought food

Chapter 7 - How to Succeed for 30 Days

Any diet change is difficult. However, with the right tools, you can succeed for 30 days and beyond. Don't look at this change to whole foods as a "diet," but rather as a philosophy you can weave into your entire life. The whole-food movement isn't about counting calories or the number on the scale - it's about healing your body from years of artificial ingredients, chemicals, and unhealthy carbs and fat. Instead of falling victim to marketing gimmicks like "fat-free," you're choosing food in its purest form, fat and all.

The best way to make the shift is to adopt a system of *inclusion* and *substitution*. This means that instead of starting from scratch, you change your diet by including more whole foods and substituting whole foods in place of processed ones. For example, start adding more vegetables to your favorite meals as sides and as part of the main entree. Here are some examples:

- Throw spinach, onions, and herbs into omelets
- Puree carrots into smoothies
- Add cooked peppers into quesadillas
- Chopped mushrooms into hamburger meat
- Mix pureed winter squash, carrots, and greens into homemade tomato sauce
- Bake thinly-sliced zucchinis and avocados for veggie fries
- Pile veggies unto homemade pizzas
- Add spinach to homemade vegan brownies

For substitution, there's really nothing that vegetables can't do when it comes to imitating less healthy ingredients. There are countless tricks and tips on the Internet about substitution, and once you get to the recipes, you'll see a score of examples there, as well. Here are some subs you can make right away:

- Whole oat groats instead of instant oats
- Fresh, whole fruit instead of fruit juice
- Fresh fish instead of canned fish
- Raw honey instead of white sugar
- Fresh produce instead of canned veggies
- Full-fat dairy instead of fat-free or low-fat dairy

- Zucchini noodles instead of lasagna pasta
- Spaghetti squash instead of spaghetti noodles
- Olive oil and vinegar instead of store-bought salad dressing
- Unsweetened, plain Greek yogurt w/ fruit instead of big-brand yogurt
- Frozen fruit puree + frozen smoothies instead of ice cream

Once you have a clearer idea about what you need to include in your diet and what you need to substitute out, you have to actually go through with it. Here are five "keys" that I believe unlock success in any diet change, and I believe they will be very helpful to you:

1. Meal prep and planning helps you avoid slip-ups

    Now, you might start out really well, and then one night you're tired and don't want to cook anything, especially since whole foods take more time than processed and packaged dishes. The solution? Plan for those nights when you're tired. This can mean doing all the measuring and chopping, and storing it in the fridge so all you have to do is throw everything in the oven or a skillet when dinnertime comes. Or, it can mean planning on having a simple spinach salad with some cold shredded chicken and cut strawberries on your busiest night, so you don't even need to turn on the stove. Anticipating those times when you don't know what to do for dinner or just don't want to cook, helps you avoid take-out temptation. Make eating whole foods just as easy as picking up the phone to order pizza or microwaving a frozen dinner.

2. Plan on making mistakes

    You will make mistakes. You will "cheat" on your whole-foods diet. By acknowledging this upfront, you are less likely to feel guilty when you eat that frozen pizza or drink that 1,000-calorie iced mocha. Of course, this does not mean that you shouldn't try your best to avoid situations where temptation lurks, but it does mean that you need to be patient with yourself. Those situations will come up, and you won't always be able to resist, but that's okay. You aren't a machine who can just be reprogrammed to only want whole foods, so don't expect that kind of discipline from yourself.

3.   Track your eating habits

Most people's eating habits are tied to their environment and emotions in some way. When you begin the 30 days eating whole foods, start a journal and track when you eat, what you eat, and why you eat. Really spend some time analyzing those times when you do slip up. Ask yourself, "Did I eat that candy bar because I was feeling frustrated with work?" "Or because I was bored and it was there?"

Keep tabs on how you eat when you're with people versus by yourself. Are there certain people who encourage you to overindulge or who give you a hard time about "dieting?" Does what you buy at the store change depending on the time of the week or day? These are just some of the questions you can ask yourself, and your answers will help you better control your environment and emotions when it comes to food.

4.   Find someone you can be accountable to

Some people are just good at being independent and motivating themselves. However, most people are not so lucky. We need encouragement and validation from others, at least in small ways. When you start your 30-day challenge, find someone who is interested in going unprocessed. Maybe it's a family member or spouse. Some people involve their whole families, so they aren't just cooking for themselves; they're cooking for their kids, too. When the challenge involves the health and wellness of others, it can be easier to get through some of the harder parts of the whole-food diet, like the longer meal prep.

There's also a sense of unity and comfort knowing that you can turn to someone when you're having a hard day. You can tell them, "I just really want ice cream right now," and they won't just spout off, "Then go have some!" You want someone who understands, but challenges you to be better.

5.   Reward yourself, but not with food

Rewarding yourself for your triumphs is an important part of a lifestyle change, but you want to avoid food as a reward. Doing something like allowing yourself a candy bar once a week if you follow the diet is not really helping you when it comes to cutting cravings. It's also a risky psychological precedent, because it tells your brain that candy bar = something good. Instead of going with bad food as a treat, go with things like a theater movie with someone special, a cool new (whole-food approved) ingredient you've never tried, a game of golf, and so on. Pick something that you like, but don't do or have very often, and make that your reward.

And that's it! Whew! You probably feel a bit overwhelmed by all the information that just got thrown at you, but there are really just three takeaways from the past seven chapters:

1) Processed food is bad.
2) Whole foods are good.
3) You can make a change to a whole-food lifestyle.

The rest of the book consists of 120 recipes for breakfast, lunch, dinner, condiments and dressings, awesome snacks (both salty and sweet!), and salads that actually fill you up. I've made them as simple as possible, from ingredient list to preparation process, so even the most amateur of home chefs can make a great-tasting dish if they follow the directions.

Chapter 8 - Breakfast

Smoked Salmon Frittata
Serves: 1-2
Time: 20-30 minutes

Frittatas are basically an egg pancake that can be customized. This version uses slices of smoked salmon and a thick, creamy green onion sauce that really takes this egg dish up a level. Frittatas take a little while to bake after you cook the eggs in the skillet, so plan ahead.

Ingredients:
4 large beaten eggs, seasoned with salt and pepper
3-4 ounces sliced smoked salmon
½ teaspoon coconut oil
1 cup coconut milk
½ cup soaked, drained, and rinsed raw cashews
¼ cup chopped green onions
1 tablespoon fresh lemon juice
1 teaspoon garlic powder
Sea salt and black pepper

Directions:
1. Begin with the green onion sauce.
2. Process the raw cashews until they are fine, and not chunky.
3. Pour in the lemon juice, coconut milk, and garlic powder.
4. Blend together until completely smooth.
5. Stir in the green onions and season with a little pepper and salt.
6. Store in the fridge so the sauce can thicken.
7. Put the coconut oil in a 10-inch skillet and melt over low heat so the pan is coated.
8. Preheat the oven to 350-degrees Fahrenheit.
9. Pour in the eggs and cook for a minute without stirring.
10. Put the skillet in the oven and cook for 10-15 minutes.

Cooking Tip:

You do NOT want to over-bake a frittata. Keep a close eye on the frittata while it's in the oven, and take it out as soon as the top starts to become a tan color. You can always cook it for a few minutes longer, you can't "uncook" it.

11. The frittata should be firm in the middle, but spongy.
12. Slide the frittata on a plate and top with the salmon and green onion sauce.

Nutritional info (per ½ frittata):
Calories: 446
Protein: 31
Carbs: 12
Fat: 31
Fiber: 1

Banana-Avocado Smoothie
Serves: 2
Time: 2 minutes

This smoothie couldn't be any easier, and it's *filling* because of the fat and fiber in the avocado. The banana keeps things sweet (but not too sweet), while the spinach adds that lovely iron and Vitamin K.

Ingredients:
1 pitted avocado
1 banana
⅓ cup spinach
¼-½ cup water

Directions:
1. Stick everything into a blender, pour in ¼ cup of water, and blend until smooth.
2. Add another ¼ cup of water if you want a thinner consistency.
3. To keep the smoothie chilled, you can also process a few cubes in with the smoothie, or freeze the banana the night before.

Nutritional info (per ½ of the total smoothie mixture):
Calories: 141
Protein: 2
Carbs: 19
Fat: 11

Fiber: 4.6

Basic Coconut-Flour Pancakes
Serves: 2
Time: 20 minutes

Mmm, pancakes. These are made with coconut flour, which is whole-food approved. Coconut flour is great because it has a naturally sweet flavor, making it perfect for baked goods. This is a basic recipe, so you can customize with fruits and nuts for variety.

Ingredients:
3 eggs
¼ cup coconut flour
⅓-¼ cup coconut milk
2 tablespoons coconut oil
⅛ cup baking soda
1-2 tablespoons raw honey
2 tablespoons organic, pure maple syrup
A little butter
Fresh fruit for garnish
A pinch of salt

Directions:
1. Whisk the coconut oil, eggs, and honey together.
2. Pour in the vanilla and coconut milk.
3. Add the baking soda, salt, and coconut flour and gently mix.
4. Prepare your skillet with a small dab of butter.
5. With a measuring cup, pour in your first pancake.
6. Depending on how big your skillet is and the size of your pancakes, you'll probably have to do a few batches.
7. You won't see a lot of bubbles on top with this recipe, so wait a few minutes before carefully checking the bottom of the pancake before flipping.
8. Serve right away, with maple syrup and any fruit you like!

Nutritional info (per ½ of the total batch and 1 tablespoon syrup each):
Calories: 382
Protein: 13
Carbs: 42
Fat: 23
Fiber: 5

Paleo Granola
Makes: 8 cups
Time: 50 minutes

A lot of whole-food recipes are also paleo, and vice versa, and while you can totally eat whole grains on the whole-food diet, it's a good idea to limit your grains in favor of veggies, fruit, nuts, and seeds. This recipe uses a wide variety of nuts with a little shredded coconut and dried cranberries.

Buying Tip:
Eden Foods has an organic dried cranberry with just three ingredients - organic cranberries, organic apple juice concentrate, and organic sunflower oil.

Ingredients:
2 cups raw cashews
2 cups raw walnuts
1 cup raw pumpkin seeds
1 cup unsweetened, shredded coconut
1 cup dried cranberries
1 lightly-beaten egg white
⅓ cup raw honey
3 tablespoons coconut oil
2 tablespoons water
1 teaspoon pure, organic vanilla extract
½ teaspoon ground cinnamon
½ teaspoon kosher salt

Directions:
1. Preheat oven to 300 degrees Fahrenheit and prepare a baking sheet with parchment paper.
2. Add the cashews, walnuts, and pumpkin seeds to a food processor and chop, but not into a meal.
3. In a separate bowl, mix the egg white with water until it's a little foamy.
4. Add the honey, vanilla, salt, cinnamon, and coconut oil (melted) to this mixture and mix well.
5. Pour the chopped nuts into this bowl, and add the coconut and cranberries.

6.   Stir.
7.   Spread the granola on the parchment paper and bake for 20-30 minutes, stirring after 10 minutes.
8.   Take out the granola and wait 10 minutes before stirring, the clusters can form.
9.   Stir gently with a spatula so the larger clusters break off from the rest of the granola.
10. Store or enjoy right away with milk or yogurt!

Nutritional info (per cup, no milk/yogurt):
Calories: 452
Protein: 34
Carbs: 28
Fat: 34
Fiber: 3.7

Classic Eggs Benedict w/ Ham
Serves: 4
Cook: 35 minutes

I love these creamy eggs in a savory ham cup, and a mouth-watering, whole-food approved Hollandaise sauce made from scratch. It's all served on a bed of fresh arugula and makes a great breakfast for a Saturday morning or brunch.

Ingredients:
8 slices organic, pasture-raised ham
8 large organic eggs
4 cups arugula
1 thinly-sliced red bell pepper
1 cup of Hollandaise sauce
Sea salt
Fresh ground pepper
½ cup grass-fed butter
3 organic egg yolks
2 tablespoons fresh lemon juice

Directions:
1.   Preheat your oven by 350-degrees Fahrenheit.
2.   Cut each piece of ham from the center to one side, making it easier to curl the ham in the muffin cup.
3.   Curl the ham pieces in a muffin tin and break an egg inside each one.

4. Season with salt and pepper before cooking in the oven for 15 minutes.
5. While these cups cook, sauté the red pepper until it becomes soft.
6. Divide the arugula and peppers on four plates.
7. To make the Hollandaise, begin by melting butter until it's very hot.
8. Quickly blend the egg yolks, lemon, and salt for 30 seconds.
9. While the blender runs, slowly add the hot butter.
10. When about half of the butter is in the blender, the sauce will start to thicken. Add the rest of the butter.
11. When the eggs are cooked, pop them out of the tin and plate two cups on top of the salad.
12. Pour on the Hollandaise and savor!

Nutritional info (per salad plate w/ 2 eggs+ham cups):
Calories: 712
Protein: 53
Carbs: 10
Fat: 117
Fiber: 1

Bacon-Cauliflower Hash

Serves: 4
Time: 25 minutes

Cauliflower is a great vegetable because it can be seasoned any way you want, and fills you up. Organic, grass-fed bacon just makes things that much better, and if you want an extra protein boost, you can serve the hash with eggs.

Ingredients:
¾ pound chopped cauliflower
6 diced slices of bacon
1 diced onion
3 tablespoons water
1 minced garlic clove
Juice from ½ lemon
2 tablespoons coconut oil
2 teaspoons minced fresh parsley
½ teaspoon paprika
Sea salt and black pepper to taste

Directions:
1. Cook the bacon in a skillet for about 10 minutes.
2. Take out the bacon, but leave the fat.
3. Add the garlic, onion, and cauliflower.
4. When they start to turn golden, add the seasonings.
5. Pour in the water and cover the skillet.
6. After about 5 minutes, the cauliflower should be fork-tender.
7. Return the bacon to the skillet and add the lemon juice.
8. Cook for 2 minutes.
9. Divide the hash among four plates and garnish with the parsley.

Nutritional info (per plate):
Calories: 58
Protein: 4.7
Carbs: 4.9
Fat: 2.3
Fiber: 1.8

Pear + Bacon Pancakes
Serves: 1
Time: 20 minutes

Pear and bacon together? In a pancake? Yes, it's true. And it is delicious. The tiny seckel pear becomes beautifully-sweet when cooked, which compliments the salt of the bacon. A little syrup or honey on top when it's cooked, and that's all the toppings you really need!

Ingredients:
4 slices organic, grass-fed bacon
2 organic eggs
2 tablespoons coconut flour
2 tablespoons almond milk
1 seckel pear
1 banana

Directions:
1. Cook the bacon until it becomes crispy.
2. Leave 2 tablespoons of grease in the pan and get rid of the rest.
3. In a blender, mix the coconut flour, banana, eggs, and milk until smooth.

4. Chop up the bacon and stir into the batter with a wooden spoon.
5. Slice the pears into ½-centimeter slices (vertical) and remove the seeds and stem.
6. Lay four of the pear slices down in the skillet (low-heat) and pour enough batter over each slice (so each pancake has one pear slice) until it covers the pear and spreads out 1-inch around. These are little pancakes.
7. Cook until the tops of the pancake start to bubble.
8. Flip the pancakes and cook until golden brown.
9. Slide the finished pancakes to a plate and use the rest of the batter for another batch.
10. Drizzle with some raw honey or organic maple syrup before enjoying.

Nutritional info (all the batter and pear slices):
Calories: 549
Protein: 25
Carbs: 68
Fat: 23
Fiber: 5

Ginger-Carrot Muffins
Serves: 12
Time: 30 minutes

These grain-free muffins taste just like carrot cake, but without all the excess sugar. Instead, they are flavored with allspice, ginger, clove, coconut, and honey, and studded with plump raisins. You'll feel energized and full after a tasty serving, and have leftovers.

Ingredients:
2 cups blanched almond flour
3 organic eggs
1 cup grated fresh carrot
¾ cup raisins (soaked for 15 minutes, then drained)
½ cup shredded, unsweetened coconut
½ cup melted coconut oil
½ cup raw honey
1-2 tablespoons fresh grated ginger
1 teaspoon baking soda
½ teaspoon sea salt
½ teaspoon powdered ginger

½ teaspoon allspice
A pinch of clove

Directions:
1. Preheat your oven to 350-degrees Fahrenheit.
2. Combine the flour, salt, spices, coconut, and baking soda in a bowl.
3. In a separate bowl, whisk the honey, coconut oil, and eggs.
4. Add the fresh ginger, raisins, and carrots.
5. Stir the wet ingredients into the dry.
6. Line a muffin tin with paper liners and spoon in the batter.
7. Bake for 24-26 minutes.
8. When you can insert a toothpick and it comes out clean, the muffins are ready.
9. Cool before either storing or enjoying right away!

Nutritional info (1-muffin serving):
Calories: 298
Protein: 6
Carbs: 25
Fat: 21
Fiber: 2

Dijon-Pork Breakfast Skillet
Serves: 4
Time: About 20 minutes

For cooler days or days you know are going to be long and hard, having a hot, hearty breakfast is especially important. This breakfast skillet is packed with pork, mushrooms, and zucchini. Seasonings like basil, garlic, and of course, Dijon mustard bring it all together into an amazing start to your day.

Ingredients:
1 pound grass-fed, organic ground pork
8 ounces of chopped fresh mushrooms
2 zucchinis cut into half-moon slices
2 tablespoons organic Dijon mustard
1 tablespoon olive oil
½ teaspoon garlic powder
½ teaspoon black pepper
½ teaspoon salt

Buying Tip:

Annie's Naturals brand sells an organic Dijon mustard made with distilled white vinegar, water, mustard seed, sea salt, clove, and other organic ingredients.

Directions:
1. Heat 1 tablespoon of oil and brown the mushrooms for 3-4 minutes.
2. Add the zucchini, season with a bit of salt and pepper, and cook for another 3-4 minutes until the zucchini is tender.
3. Move the veggies to the side so the middle part of the pan is available.
4. Add the pork and spices.
5. Using a spatula or wooden spoon, break up the meat and brown, not stirring in the veggies.
6. When the meat is cooked through, then you can mix the mushrooms and zucchini.
7. Add the Dijon mustard and stir until it's heated through.
8. Season again to your liking before dividing up the hash between four plates.

Nutritional info (per 1 plate serving):
Calories: 278
Protein: 34
Carbs: 4
Fat: 14
Fiber: 3

Sweet Potato Quiche w/ Bacon and Spinach
Serves: 4
Time: 1 hour, 15 minutes

Sweet potatoes are a great ingredient because they can be served sweet, spicy, or salty. In this quiche, they serve as the sweet crust, and are filled with protein-rich eggs, salty bacon, and fresh spinach.

Ingredients:
4 peeled sweet potatoes cut into very thin rounds
5 beaten organic eggs
2 cups fresh spinach

3 cooked and crumbled bacon slices
1 sliced onion
1 minced garlic clove
2 tablespoons fresh chives
2 teaspoons olive oil
Coconut oil (for cooking)
Sea salt and ground pepper to taste

Directions:
1. Preheat your oven to 400 degrees and place the potato slices in a pie dish, so they create a circular "crust" around the edges and bottom of the dish.
2. Season with olive oil, pepper, and salt.
3. Bake in the oven for 15-20 minutes.
4. In the meantime, sauté the garlic and onion in a skillet with some coconut oil.
5. Cook for about 5 minutes before adding the spinach.
6. Once the spinach has wilted (2-3 minutes), remove from the heat.
7. When the crust is done, reduce the oven heat to 375-degrees.
8. In a separate bowl, mix the eggs with the contents of your skillet, the crumbled and cooked bacon, and chives.
9. Pour this over the crust to fill.
10. Bake for 30-35 minutes until the eggs are set.

Nutritional info (¼ of the quiche per serving):
Calories: 257
Protein: 12
Carbs: 30
Fat: 11
Fiber: 7

Raw Cranberry-Coconut-Cashew Fig Bars
Serves: 20
Time: 20 minutes

These are great for people on-the-go who don't have time to cook a hot meal every morning. They're organic energy bars, with the main source of their sweetness and fiber coming from the Black Mission figs, which are known for their natural, intense flavor that's almost like liquor. The bars also pretty easy to make - you just process everything, stick in the fridge for a few hours, and cut! No baking required!

Ingredients:
2 cups unsweetened, shredded coconut
1 cup raw, unsalted cashews
1 cup dried cranberries
1 cup dried Black Mission figs
2 tablespoons honey
1 tablespoon coconut oil
½ teaspoon cinnamon
½ teaspoon sea salt

Directions:
1. Mix all the ingredients (except the cashews and honey) in a food processor.
2. While the processor runs, pour in the honey through the tube.
3. Quickly pulse the cashews through the mixture.
4. Line an 8x8 pan with oven paper and then press the bar "batter" into the pan, so it's firm and even.
5. Refrigerate for 2 hours before cutting into 20 squares.
6. Store in the fridge with saran-wrap over the pan.

Nutritional info (1 square per serving):
Calories: 116
Protein: 6
Carbs: 15
Fat: 6
Fiber: 3

Broccoli Spinach Frittata

Serves: 4
Time: 40 minutes

This frittata is a great way to get in your veggies, specifically those of the dark, green, and leafy variety. The eggs are a perfect vehicle for the broccoli and spinach, and flavors like oregano, onion, and sea salt keep everything tasting fresh.

Ingredients:
6 beaten organic eggs
4 cups chopped broccoli florets
4 cups chopped fresh baby spinach
4 minced garlic cloves

2 tablespoons grass-fed butter
1 onion chopped into half rings
½ teaspoon unrefined sea salt
¼ teaspoon dried oregano

Directions:
1. Preheat the oven to 350-degrees and steam the broccoli in a steamer basket for 5 minutes.
2. When the broccoli is bright green, rinse with cold water.
3. In a skillet, melt the butter and sauté the onion rings until they are caramelized. This should take about 20-25 minutes.
4. Add the minced garlic to the skillet and cook for another minute.
5. Add the spinach with the salt and wilt.
6. Rinse and drain the broccoli before adding to the skillet, along with the oregano.
7. Stir until all the veggies are mixed well.
8. Pour over the beaten eggs and gently shake the pan, so the eggs settle evenly.
9. Bake for 20-25 minutes.
10. Serve and enjoy!

Nutritional info (¼ frittata per serving):
Calories: 265
Protein: 18
Carbs: 17
Fat: 14
Fiber: 4

Chile Relleno Casserole
Serves: 6
Time: 55 minutes

"Chile relleno" is a Spanish dish, which translates to, "stuffed chile." It originally consisted of a green chile stuffed with meat and then coated with eggs. This is an easier variation, where all the flavors of chile relleno - pork, egg, green chiles, and chipotle seasoning - are still retained, but in a much simpler method.

Ingredients:
12-ounces pasture-raised ground pork
10-12 sliced organic button mushrooms
10 beaten organic eggs

¾ cup diced white onion
9-10 whole green chiles
1 tablespoon grass-fed butter
½ teaspoon garlic powder
½ teaspoon sea salt
¼ teaspoon ground coriander
¼ teaspoon smoked paprika
Pinch of ground chipotle pepper
Pinch of black pepper

Directions:
1. Preheat the oven to 350-degrees and melt the butter in a skillet over medium-high.
2. Using your hand, mix the ground pork and dry spices together before browning in the pan for 5 minutes.
3. In the meantime, prepare the mushrooms and onions.
4. Add them to the pork.
5. Cook for 5 minutes.
6. Remove from the heat.
7. Slice the green chiles horizontally, so they have a flat side.
8. Place 4-5 chiles in a baking dish, and then layer on half of the pork. Add the rest of the chiles, and then rest of the pork mixture.
9. Pour the whisked eggs over the top and let it settle.
10. Cover the dish and bake for 40 minutes.
11. You can serve as is, or with some fresh salsa or avocado!

Nutritional info (⅙ casserole per serving):
Calories: 288
Protein: 19.6
Carbs: 15.2
Fat: 17.3
Fiber: 1

Banana-Nut Porridge
Serves: 4
Time: 10 minutes (not counting overnight cashew soak)

Who doesn't love a banana-nut muffin? They're delicious, but they also take time to bake, and they're not the healthiest breakfast in the world. So, let's transform it into a porridge! This recipe uses *three* kinds of nuts - cashews, almonds, and pecans - and coconut milk for a smooth, creamy taste.

Ingredients:
1 very ripe banana
2 cups coconut milk
½ cup raw pecans
½ cup raw cashews
½ cup raw almonds
2 teaspoons cinnamon
A pinch of sea salt

Directions:
1. The night before you plan on eating the porridge, fill a bowl with filtered water and add a little sea salt.
2. Put all the nuts in this bowl, so they're covered by at least 1-inch of water, and cover.
3. The next morning, drain the nuts and rinse 2-3 times.
4. Put the nuts in a food processor and blend with the banana, cinnamon, and coconut milk until smooth.
5. Divide into four bowls and microwave for 40 seconds each.
6. Serve hot!

Nutritional info (1 bowl per serving):
Calories: 317.5
Protein: 7.25
Carbs: 18
Fat: 26.25
Fiber: 4

Almond-Peach Chia Pudding
Serves: 4
Time: Overnight (after 5-minute prep)

Chia seeds are an amazing food. They are low in calories and super high in nutrients, including fiber, protein, and antioxidants. When you soak them overnight in coconut milk, they plump up, making a delicious pudding. For this recipe, you finish off the pudding with toasted almonds and fresh sliced peaches.

Ingredients:
28-ounces of coconut milk (not Goya)
Two large, fresh peaches
½ cup sliced, toasted almonds
¼ cup chia seeds

irections:
1. Pour both cans of coconut milk in a medium-sized bowl and stir to mix in any coconut cream that separated in the can.
2. Stir in the chia seeds.
3. Cover and store in the fridge overnight.
4. The next morning, divide the pudding into four bowls and add sliced peaches and toasted almonds.
5. Add a little coconut milk if the pudding is too thick for your liking.

Nutritional info (1 bowl per serving):
Calories: 223
Protein: 7
Carbs: 17
Fat: 16
Fiber: 12

Maple Breakfast Scotch Eggs

Serves: 8
Time: 30 minutes

Scotch eggs are when you hard-boil an egg, peel it, and then wrap it in sausage meat and bake it. The result is a tasty protein bomb. This recipe uses organic ground pork sweetened with pure maple syrup. If you like hard-boiled eggs with a gooey yolk, you should boil them for about 6 minutes before peeling and wrapping in meat.

Ingredients:
1 pound organic, pasture-raised ground pork
8 hard-boiled eggs
1 ½ teaspoons pure maple syrup
½ teaspoon sea salt
½ teaspoon black pepper

Directions:
1. Preheat the oven to 375-degrees.
2. In a bowl, combine the ground pork with maple syrup, sea salt, and black pepper.
3. Divide up the meat into 8 patties.
4. Take a peeled egg and shape the patty completely around the egg. Repeat until all the patties and eggs are used.
5. Bake the scotch eggs for 25 minutes.

6. Cool for 5 minutes before enjoying.

Nutritional info (1 scotch egg per serving):
Calories: 403
Protein: 38
Carbs: 18
Fat: 20.8
Fiber: 0

Prosciutto-Wrapped Mini Frittata Muffins
Serves: 6
Time: 30 minutes

It's important to have portable breakfast options for those days when you have no time to really "cook." You can make these mini frittata muffins during the evening, and then have 12 mini muffins for the rest of the week.

Ingredients:
8 big eggs
½ pound thinly-sliced cremini mushrooms
½ pound frozen, organic spinach
5-ounces of Prosciutto
3 minced garlic cloves
½ finely-diced onion
1 cup halved cherry tomatoes
¼ cup full-fat coconut milk
4 tablespoons coconut oil
2 tablespoons coconut flour
Pinch of sea salt
Pinch of black pepper

Directions:
1. Preheat your oven to 375-degrees.
2. In a skillet, heat half of the coconut oil and sauté your onion until it becomes translucent.
3. Add the mushrooms and garlic until the liquid from the mushrooms has evaporated.
4. Season with salt and pepper, and remove from heat.
5. In a separate bowl, beat the eggs with coconut flour, coconut milk, and more salt and pepper.
6. Spoon in the mushrooms and spinach, and mix.

7. Prepare the muffin tin with a little coconut oil and line with prosciutto.
8. Pour in the frittata batter and top with halved cherry tomatoes.
9. Cook for 20 minutes, rotating the muffin tin 18-degrees 10 minutes in.
10. Cool before serving or storing.

Nutritional info (2 mini muffins per serving):
Calories: 290
Protein: 18
Carbs: 11
Fat: 20
Fiber: 3

Apple Skillet Pancake
Serves: 6 people
Time: About an hour

This baked pancake is kind of like a Dutch Baby, but much healthier and lighter. It is a great breakfast during autumn, when apples are in season, or even as a dessert following a brunch.

Ingredients:
6 organic eggs
4 medium-sized organic apples
½ cup coconut milk
¼ cup coconut flour
¼ cup melted coconut oil
2 tablespoons cinnamon
2 tablespoons of honey
1 teaspoon pure organic vanilla extract
1 teaspoon lemon juice
¼ teaspoon sea salt

Directions:
1. Preheat your oven to 375-degrees.
2. Prepare the apples by removing the cores and slicing them very thin. Set a handful aside for the topping.
3. Heat the coconut oil in a skillet (preferably cast-iron) and sauté the apples until they are slightly soft.
4. Add the salt, cinnamon, lemon juice, and honey/vanilla (mix these two together before adding) and mix to coat the apples.

5.	In another bowl, whisk the eggs and add the coconut milk and coconut flour.
6.	Pour the batter on top of the cooked apples and top with the set-aside, uncooked apple slices.
7.	Put the skillet into the oven and bake for 40 minutes.
8.	The pancake is ready when the top is golden and puffy.

Nutritional info (⅙ of the pancake per serving):
Calories: 253
Protein: 7
Carbs: 25
Fat: 13
Fiber: 5

Paleo Tropical Granola
Serves: 7
Time: About 2.5 hours

This time around, our granola recipe comes courtesy of the tropics. It's packed with fresh pineapple, dates, macadamia nuts, and raw coconut flakes. Sweeteners like fresh orange juice add even more sunshine to this grainless cereal, so you're guaranteed to feel bright and alert when you eat it.

Ingredients:
5 pitted and chopped Medjool dates
3 cups raw coconut flakes
3 cups chopped raw almonds
1 cup chopped raw macadamia nuts
1 cup cubed fresh pineapple
½ cup raw sunflower seeds
½ cup melted coconut oil
2 tablespoons orange juice
1 tablespoon pure organic vanilla extract
1 teaspoon ground cinnamon
½ teaspoon sea salt

Directions:
1.	Preheat the oven to 250-degrees and prepare two baking sheets with oven paper.
2.	In a food processor, blend the pineapple, vanilla, orange juice, and cinnamon until liquefied.
3.	Add the melted coconut oil and blend again.

4. In a separate bowl, mix the almonds, macadamia nuts, coconut flakes, salt, and seeds with your hands.
5. Add the wet mixture on top of the dry and mix.
6. Divide the granola between the two baking sheets and spread into a thin layer.
7. Bake in the oven for 2 hours.
8. Toss every 20 minutes and rotate the baking sheets halfway through the baking cycle, so the granola bakes evenly.
9. Cool before eating or storing.

Nutritional info (1 cup per serving):
Calories: 588
Protein: 2
Carbs: 29
Fat: 53
Fiber: 17

Bacon-Avocado Muffins

Serves: 12
Time: 30 minutes

Muffins don't have to be sweet. Sometimes, they can be savory, and they are awesome, like these bacon-avocado beauties. Ingredients like creamy avocado and coconut milk keep the muffins moist, while bacon adds a spark of saltiness and protein.

Ingredients:
6 short-cut bacon strips
4 eggs
1 small onion
2 cups mashed avocado
1 cup coconut milk
½ cup coconut flour
½ teaspoon baking soda
Salt and pepper
Coconut oil

Directions:
1. Preheat the oven to 350-degrees.
2. Prepare the muffin pan by wiping the insides with melted coconut oil.
3. Dice the onion and bacon.
4. Brown in a pan.

5. In the meantime, mix the avocado and eggs together with a fork.
6. Add the coconut milk.
7. Next, add the baking soda, salt, pepper, and coconut flour.
8. Mix well so it's completely smooth.
9. Fold in ¾ of the onion-bacon mixture.
10. Pour in the muffin tin and top with the last ¼ of the bacon/onion.
11. Bake for 20 minutes.
12. Cool before enjoying!

Nutritional info (1 muffin per serving):
Calories: 111
Protein: 5
Carbs: 6
Fat: 8
Fiber: 3

Butternut Squash Porridge
Serves: 4
Time: About 1 hour

Butternut squash is sweet, but most people don't know how to use it in desserts or breakfasts. Instead of grains, the squash serves as the body of the porridge, embracing the natural sweet flavors of butternut squash and combines it with full-fat coconut milk, fresh fruit, and toasted shredded coconut. You can decide on how much honey to use if the squash isn't quite sweet enough to your liking.

Ingredients:
1 medium-sized butternut squash
1 can full-fat, chilled coconut milk
1 cup fresh raspberries
½ cup shredded, toasted coconut
Honey to taste
Cinnamon to taste

Directions:
1. Preheat the oven to 350-degrees.
2. Cut the squash in half lengthwise, and place cut-side down on a greased cookie sheet.
3. Bake for 1 hour or until you can easily pierce the inside flesh with a fork.

4. Wait until you can touch the squash, but it's still warm.
5. Scoop out the seeds, and then the flesh.
6. Divide up the flesh into four bowls and mash to your desired consistency.
7. Sweeten with honey.
8. Pour an equal amount of coconut milk into each bowl.
9. Top with coconut, fresh raspberries, and cinnamon.

Nutritional info (1 bowl per serving):
Calories: 150
Protein: 2
Carbs: 23
Fat: 7
Fiber: 2.7

Homemade Breakfast Sausage
Serves: 4
Time: 12 minutes

Breakfast sausage is one of the most processed foods out there, so why not make your own? It's extremely easy and only uses a few ingredients. You can make a huge batch and freeze the raw sausage, too, and have breakfasts for weeks.

Ingredients:
½ pound of pasture-raised, organic ground pork
1 tablespoons dried chives
1 teaspoon dried garlic powder
1 teaspoon dried onion powder
1 teaspoon dried mustard
½ teaspoon sea salt

Directions:
1. Heat a skillet with a little coconut oil.
2. Mix the meat and spices together and form 8 mini patties.
3. Cook for 12 minutes on medium-high until done.
4. Serve with eggs or any other favorite breakfast items.

Nutritional info (2 patties per serving):
Calories: 121
Protein: 17
Carbs: 1
Fat: 6

Fiber: 0

Blueberry-Banana Chia Pudding
Serves: 4
Time: 30 minutes

Here's another recipe for chia pudding! Chia pudding is kind of like oatmeal in how you can customize it anyway you like. This version is also very fast and can be eaten after only 30 minutes of soaking.

Ingredients:
5 large dates (if they're hard, soak in hot water)
2 cups fresh blueberries
⅔ cup almond milk
½ frozen banana
½ cup chia seeds

Directions:
1. Puree the milk, dates, banana, and blueberries in a blender.
2. Move to a bowl and stir in the chia seeds.
3. Stick in the fridge for 30 minutes.
4. Divide pudding into four bowls and enjoy!

Nutritional info (1 bowl per serving):
Calories: 212
Protein: 5
Carbs: 42
Fat: 6
Fiber: 6

Baked Tomatoes
Serves: 2
Time: 30 minutes

Tomatoes make great cups that you can fill with just about anything. For this breakfast, you stuff a tomato with spinach and then crack an egg on top for a meal that's rich in protein and antioxidants. It's a great way to start the day.

Ingredients:
6 tomatoes
6 eggs
2 cups baby spinach

Sea salt

Directions:
1. Preheat your oven to 390-degrees.
2. Cut off the top of the tomatoes and scoop out the insides.
3. Place the hollowed-out tomatoes in a ceramic baking dish that's been greased.
4. Fill about ¾ of the way with baby spinach.
5. Add a dash of sea salt to each tomato before cracking an egg over the spinach into the tomato.
6. Bake for 20-30 minutes until the egg is cooked through.
7. Crack on some fresh black pepper and enjoy!

Nutritional info (1 stuffed tomato per serving):
Calories: 114
Protein: 9
Carbs: 3
Fat: 7
Fiber: 2

Breakfast Meatloaf
Serves: 4-5
Time: 57 minutes

Meatloaf - it isn't just for dinner anymore. This meaty breakfast (made with both ground beef *and* pork sausage) is packed with veggies like zucchinis and mushrooms, and is perfect for cold winter mornings when you need something hot. You can make this the night before (since it does take close to an hour) and have leftovers for the next few mornings.

Ingredients:
1 pound grass-fed ground beef
10-12 ounces of organic (or homemade organic) pork breakfast sausage
4 ounces of sliced button mushrooms
2 minced garlic cloves
1 diced zucchini
1 diced yellow onion
2 tablespoons dried basil
2 tablespoons dried parsley
1 tablespoon grass-fed butter
1 teaspoon garlic powder

Sea salt and black pepper to taste

<u>Directions:</u>
1. Preheat your oven to 400-degrees.
2. On the stove, heat the butter and sauté the garlic and onions over medium-high in a skillet.
3. When the onions are translucent, add the zucchini.
4. Cover the skillet to steam the squash.
5. After 3-4 minutes, add the mushrooms and cover again for another 4-5 minutes.
6. When the veggies are soft, throw in the basil, parsley, garlic powder, sea salt, and pepper.
7. Mix and then remove from the heat.
8. Once cool, move to a bowl and mix with the meat using your hands.
9. Prepare a big bread pan with foil and firmly pack a loaf with the meat mixture in the pan.
10. Bake for 40-45 minutes.
11. Wait 10 minutes before serving.

<u>Nutritional info (¼ the meatloaf per serving):</u>
Calories: 374
Protein: 25
Carbs: 6
Fat: 28
Fiber: 1

Cinnamon Squash + Beef-Stuffed Bell Peppers
Serves: 4
Time: 50 minutes

Since these stuffed peppers take close to an hour, they are a great option for a lazy Sunday breakfast or brunch. The time it takes is totally worth it, though. Juicy bell peppers are filled with cinnamon-spiced butternut squash and ground beef, along with crushed walnuts and onion. You'll feel all warm and cozy inside after eating one of these guys.

<u>Ingredients:</u>
4 large bell peppers (yellow or red)
½ pound grass-fed, pasture-raised ground beef
2 cups cubed butternut squash
½ diced onion

½ cup crushed walnuts
1 egg
2 teaspoons cardamom
2 teaspoons cinnamon
Sea salt
Coconut oil (for cooking)

Directions:
1. Preheat your oven to 350-degrees.
2. Hollow out the bell peppers. You may have to cut a bit off the bottom, so the pepper can stand on its own.
3. Bake in the oven for 40 minutes on a tray.
4. In the meantime, heat 1 tablespoon of coconut oil and sauté the butternut squash for 5 minutes.
5. Next, add the onions.
6. In another pan, brown the ground beef (in another tablespoon of oil).
7. Crack an egg into the meat and mix.
8. When the onions are clear, add the whole skillet (onions + squash) into the meat pan.
9. Mix in the walnuts, cardamom, cinnamon, and salt.
10. Cook until the squash is easily pierced with a fork.
11. The peppers should be out of the oven by now, so stuff with the squash/meat mixture.
12. Enjoy!

Nutritional info (1 stuffed pepper per serving):
Calories: 309
Protein: 22
Carbs: 24
Fat: 15
Fiber: 5

Omelet Cupcakes
Serves: 5
Time: About 30 minutes

These are omelets in bite form and the perfect portable breakfast. They include all the usual omelet goodies - bacon, spinach, tomato, onion, and bell peppers.

Ingredients:
8 eggs

5 slices of bacon
1 big chopped bell pepper
1 small chopped white onion
1 cup chopped fresh spinach
1 cup halved cherry tomatoes
Sea salt and pepper to taste

Directions:
1. Preheat the oven to 350-degrees.
2. In a skillet, cook the bacon until nearly done and remove. The bacon will finish cooking in the oven.
3. Add the chopped veggies into the same skillet as the bacon and sauté in the leftover grease.
4. In a separate bowl, crack and whisk the eggs with salt and pepper.
5. Cut up the bacon and add to the veggie skillet.
6. Distribute the veggie/bacon mix into a cupcake pan (preferably lined with silicone baking cups) and pour over the egg mixture.
7. Bake for 17 minutes until the eggs set.
8. Eat right away and store the leftovers in the fridge.

Nutritional info (2 omelet bites per serving):
Calories: 182
Protein: 14
Carbs: 5
Fat: 13
Fiber: 1

Steel-Cut Oats w/ Berry Compote
Serves: 4
Time: 30 minutes

Steel-cut oats are nuttier than regular oatmeal, and it can be refrigerated for up to a week, which you could never do with regular oatmeal that gets too mushy. Steel-cut oats are also unrefined, so they retain more of their nutritional value. This recipe serves the oats with a warm mixed-berry compote that is to die for.

Ingredients:
3 cups of water
1 cup steel-cut oats
⅛ teaspoon salt

12-ounces of organic frozen mixed berries
2 tablespoons honey
2 teaspoons fresh lemon juice
1 teaspoon grass-fed butter
Dash of cinnamon

Directions:
1. Start by making the steel-oats, since that takes the majority of the cooking time.
2. Bring 3 cups of water to a boil in a saucepan.

> **Cooking Tip:**
>
> If you prefer creamier oatmeal, increase the water to 4 cups.

3. Stir in the salt and oats into the water.
4. Return the saucepan to a rolling boil.
5. Reduce the heat and simmer for 20-30 minutes, occasionally stirring.
6. When there's about 10 minutes left for the oatmeal, make the compote.
7. Melt the butter in a separate saucepan before adding the rest of the ingredients in the second list (berries, lemon juice, etc.).
8. Bring to a boil, and then reduce.
9. Simmer for 5 minutes.
10. When the oatmeal is ready, divide up into 4 bowls, and then distribute the compote.

Nutritional info (1 bowl w/ compote per serving):
Calories: 107
Protein: 2
Carbs: 20
Fat: 2
Fiber: 5

Protein Monster Breakfast Cookies
Serves: 16-20
Time: 25 minutes

Healthy cookies are one of my favorite go-to breakfasts, because they are super portable and can pack in a lot of nutritious ingredients. This recipe for "monster" cookies includes almond butter, flax meal, and hemp seed for health, and raisins, maple syrup, shredded coconut, and 70% cocoa chocolate chips for deliciousness! Note that this recipe also includes palm sugar, which is a natural sweetener made from the sap of the date palm.

Ingredients:
1 cup almond butter
⅓ cup hemp seeds
⅓ cup raisins
⅓ cup palm sugar
⅔ cup unsweetened, shredded coconut
¼ cup pure maple syrup
¼ cup 70% organic chocolate chips
3 tablespoons boiling water
1 tablespoon flax meal
1 teaspoon pure organic vanilla extract
½ teaspoon baking soda
¼ teaspoon sea salt

Directions:
1. Preheat the oven to 350-degrees and prepare two baking sheets with oven paper.
2. Stir the boiling water and flax meal together and set aside for 10 minutes.
3. In the meantime, cream the sugar, maple syrup, vanilla, and almond butter together.
4. Beat the baking soda and sea salt in.
5. Stir in the rest of the ingredients, including the flax meal/water mix.
6. Using a tablespoon measurement, roll the dough into balls and space them 3-inches apart on the baking sheets.
7. Using your finger, flatten the dough to ½-inch thickness.
8. Bake for 12-14 minutes until the edges are golden-brown.
9. Cool before eating.
10. For storage, you should keep them out on the counter, uncovered, or they will become mushy.

Nutritional info (1 cookie per serving):
Calories: 135
Protein: 4
Carbs: 14
Fat: 9

Fiber: 2

Monkey Salad
Serves: 1
Time: 5 minutes

This is probably the fastest, easiest breakfast you could make that still has good nutritional value. You can even toss it into a Tupperware and eat it on the way to work if you have to.

Ingredients:
1 peeled and sliced banana
1 handful raw cashews
1 handful unsweetened coconut flakes

Directions:
1.   Layer everything in a bowl, without stirring.
2.   Eat!

Nutritional info (1 bowl per serving):
Calories: 310
Protein: 5
Carbs: 37
Fat: 17
Fiber: 3

Chapter 9 - Lunch

Garden Ratatouille w/ Poached Eggs
Serves: 3
Time: 40 minutes

If you love Pixar movies, you're probably thinking, "Oh! Ratatouille! Like the rat!" *Actually*, the rat's name was Remy, and he made ratatouille. And now, so will you! This layered vegetable dish makes an awesome brunch or lunch that's bursting with flavor and nutrients. It also freezes really well (without the egg, of course), so you can make a lot and eat it whenever you want!

Ingredients:
½ cup all-natural, organic (or homemade) chicken stock
¼ cup chopped fresh parsley
6 peeled, seeded, and chopped tomatoes
4 minced garlic cloves
3 poached eggs
1 diced medium eggplant
2 diced zucchini
1 diced red bell pepper
1 diced onion
1 diced green bell pepper
1 diced jalapeno
2 tablespoons tomato paste
2 tablespoons grass-fed butter
2 tablespoons fresh thyme
1 tablespoon fresh oregano
Salt and pepper to taste
Olive oil

Directions:
1. Heat the butter in a skillet and sauté the onions for about 5 minutes.
2. Next, add the eggplant and sauté for 10 minutes.
3. Add the tomato paste until it turns to a dull red or brick color.
4. Toss in the chopped tomatoes and cook for 5-7 minutes.
5. Add the herbs, zucchini, garlic, and peppers and stir.

in the chicken broth and put the lid on the skillet.
down the heat and simmer for 20 minutes or until the
h has evaporated.
8. Divide the veggies among three plates, and add salt and pepper to your liking.
9. Top each plate with a poached egg and drizzle of olive oil.

<u>Nutritional info (1 plate per serving):</u>
Calories: 318
Protein: 13
Carbs: 29
Fat: 18
Fiber: 4.6

Chipotle-Chicken Lettuce Tacos
Serves: 3
Time: 30 minutes

Tacos make a great lunch because they are easy to pack and don't take much assembly. This recipe uses crisp lettuce instead of a tortilla or taco shell, so you reduce the number of calories the meal has, and you're getting more nutrients from the lettuce. The chipotle chicken is really the star here, and is seasoned to perfection with homemade pickled jalapeno chillies (see the recipe in chapter 11), cumin, brown sugar, and so on.

<u>Ingredients:</u>
1 pound skinless thinly-sliced chicken breasts
4 big butter lettuce leaves
1 finely-sliced red onion
2 chopped tomatoes
1 teaspoon ground chipotle
½ teaspoon cumin
A handful of fresh coriander leaves
Sliced, pickled jalapeno chillies to taste
Brown sugar to taste
Salt and pepper to taste
Olive oil (for cooking)
1 sliced avocado
Lime wedges

For salsa:
1 cup quartered cherry tomatoes

1 cup sliced red onion
Salt and pepper to taste

Directions:
1. Heat the olive oil in a pan and fry the chicken pieces to a golden hue.
2. Remove the chicken and sauté the onion in the pan until soft.
3. Put the tomatoes, sugar, cumin, and chipotle in the pan and simmer for 15-25 minutes. The sauce should thicken around the pan's edges.
4. Put the chicken back into the pan and cook for 5 minutes.
5. Arrange the taco toppings (avocado, pickled jalapeno, salsa) in bowls so people can make their own.
6. Before serving the chicken, add a healthy spritz of fresh lime juice.
7. Bring out the lettuce leaves and assemble!

Nutritional info (1 lettuce taco w/ salsa + toppings per serving):
Calories: 461
Protein: 52.1
Carbs: 27.9
Fat: 20.2
Fiber: 4.3

Egg-Roll-In-A-Bowl
Serves: 4
Time: 15 minutes

Chinese food is a definite "no" if you are going for whole foods. There are very few restaurants that don't use artificial ingredients like MSG, so you'll have to make your own dishes. Luckily, meals like this eggroll in bowl form are super easy and just as delicious. You can add any kind of meat to this as well, if you like, such as chicken, sautéed shrimp, or beef.

Ingredients:
16-ounces cooked chicken breast
1 medium chopped head of cabbage
1 large sliced carrot
4 diced green onions
⅓ cup coconut aminos
1 tablespoon sesame oil

1 tablespoon coconut oil

Eating Tip:

Coconut aminos is an alternative to soy sauce and is made from the aged sap of coconut blossoms with salt.

Directions:
1. Heat the coconut oil in a skillet.
2. Add the cabbage and carrot, and sauté until soft.
3. Pour in the sesame oil and coconut aminos.
4. Sauté a few more minutes until most of the liquid is absorbed.
5. Toss in the green onions and 16-ounces of cooked chicken breast, or the cooked meat of your choice.
6. Heat through, and then distribute among three plates.

Nutritional info (1 plate per serving):
Calories: 338
Protein: 35
Carbs: 8
Fat: 11
Fiber: 5

Chilled Herb-Poached Salmon
Serves: 4
Time: 3 hours, 17 minutes (17 minute cook time)

This salmon is for lunch, because it's meant to be served cold. You can cook it the night before and chill it in the fridge before heading off to work the next morning. Buying salmon fillets can be tricky, because they come in such different sizes and thicknesses, so for this recipe, aim for about ¼ pound per person, and get one pound of salmon fillets.

Ingredients:
1 pound salmon fillets
4 cups of water
¼ cup fresh chopped parsley
3 chopped garlic cloves
1 chopped onion
2 lemons (one juiced, one sliced)

2 big tablespoons fresh chopped tarragon
2 tablespoons olive oil
1 tablespoon fresh chopped thyme
Lots of sea salt and pepper

Directions:
1. Sauté the garlic and onion in hot olive oil in a skillet.
2. When they are soft, add the rest of the herbs and lemons.
3. After cooking for a few minutes, pour in the salt, pepper, and water.
4. Bring to a boil and then simmer for 15 minutes.
5. Put the fish in the liquid (make sure it is covered), with the skin side facing down.
6. Let the fish rest there for 8-12 minutes. The fish should be 145-degrees Fahrenheit to be safe. Be gentle when you're pushing in the thermometer.
7. When the fish is ready, carefully move the fish to a tray and slide a spatula between the salmon and skin to remove the skin.
8. Store in the fridge for at least 3 hours before eating.
9. Serve atop a simple salad of fresh greens, cherry tomatoes, and cucumbers.

Nutritional info (¼ pound salmon per serving):
Calories: 329
Protein: 24
Carbs: 9
Fat: 22
Fiber: 0

California Turkey-Bacon Lettuce Wraps
Serves: 2
Time: About 11-15 minutes

A classic deli sandwich goes breadless. These awesome lettuce wraps include turkey, avocado, tomato, and *bacon*. They are also super fast to make - the only real cooking is the bacon, and the whole wrap comes together with a fantastic basil mayo, though you can put any spread you want on the lettuce. For more mayo and condiments ideas, head over to Chapter 11.

Ingredients:
1 head iceberg lettuce

4 slices all-natural deli turkey (Applegate Farms is a good brand)
4 slices organic bacon
1 thinly-sliced tomato
1 thinly-sliced avocado
6 large, torn basil leaves
½ cup homemade mayonnaise (see Chapter 11)
1 chopped garlic clove
1 teaspoon lemon juice
Salt and pepper to taste

Directions:
1. For the basil-mayo, mix the ingredients in the second list in a food processor until smooth.
2. Lay 1 slice of turkey on two layers of lettuce leaves.
3. Spread on some mayo (about ½ tablespoon), followed by another slice of turkey, bacon, and then some avocado and tomato. You won't use all the mayo, save the rest for later.
4. Season with salt and pepper.
5. Roll the bottom of the leaves up and fold the sides in, like a burrito.
6. Cut in half and eat!

Nutritional info (2 lettuce wrap halves per serving):
Calories: 424
Protein: 29
Carbs: 13
Fat: 30
Fiber: 1

Skillet Butternut Squash w/ Greens and Bacon
Serves: 5
Time: 15 minutes

This quick lunch could also serve as a tasty side dish, but it does have all the elements of a great midday meal - protein, veggies, and little work. The recipe makes enough for five people, so you can save some for later if you're making it just for yourself.

Ingredients:
1 pound diced bacon
1 medium peeled, seeded, and cubed butternut squash (about 2 pounds)
1 diced zucchini

1 bunch diced chard
Olive oil
Balsamic vinegar

Directions:
1. Cover your prepared butternut squash in water in a large pan and bring to a boil.
2. You should boil the squash for 5-7 minutes until it is fork-tender, but not mushy.
3. In the meantime, cook the bacon in another skillet.
4. When the squash is ready, drain out the water and add to the skillet with the bacon.
5. Throw in the zucchini and chard, as well.
6. Sauté until the chard wilts.
7. Drizzle with balsamic vinegar and olive oil just before serving.

Nutritional info (⅕ skillet per serving):
Calories: 593
Protein: 35
Carbs: 25
Fat: 39
Fiber: 10

Chicken Burrito Bowl
Serves: 4
Time: About an hour (not counting overnight marinate)

This is a no-fuss, hearty lunch that's perfect for days when you're craving a burrito, but don't want to mess up your whole-food diet. You just marinate and grill some chicken the night before, and then assemble the bowl when you're ready to eat, with Pico de Gallo and brown rice flavored with cilantro. There's a lot of ingredients, but it's actually very easy to put together.

Ingredients:
2-3 pounds of boneless, skinless organic chicken thighs
2 garlic cloves
¼ cup olive oil
1 tablespoon apple cider vinegar
1 tablespoon chipotle chili powder
1 tablespoon fresh lime juice
2 teaspoons sea salt

1 teaspoon paprika
1 teaspoon black pepper
½ teaspoon dried oregano
2 cups cooked brown rice
¼ cup chopped fresh cilantro
1 tablespoon fresh lime juice
2 teaspoons avocado oil
1 teaspoon lemon juice
½ teaspoon sea salt
1 large diced tomato
½ diced small onion
¼ cup fresh chopped cilantro
1 tablespoon fresh lime juice
½ teaspoon sea salt

Directions:
1. To save time, you should make the chicken the night before.
2. Mix all the ingredients after the chicken thighs (first list of ingredients) in a blender until smooth.
3. Add the chicken and marinade in a Ziploc bag and refrigerate at least 30 minutes. The longer the better.
4. Grill the chicken, letting it rest for 5 minutes before you chop it up. The grilling process should take about 10-15 minutes. You can also cook the chicken in the oven or stovetop if you want.
5. Divide the cut chicken into four equal parts and store in plastic containers or Ziploc bags overnight.
6. The night before is also a good time to cook the rice.
7. The next morning, it's time to make the rice and Pico de Gallo.
8. For the Pico, you will need at least 20 minutes. Season the tomato and let it drain in a colander for 20 minutes.
9. Mix the tomato with the rest of the ingredients in the third list and set aside.
10. For the rice, mix the avocado oil in with the cooked brown rice.
11. Add the citrus juices and salt, and stir.
12. Lastly, add the cilantro.
13. You can store ¼ of the rice and Pico in the same container as the cooked chicken if you like, or take separate Tupperware boxes and create your bowl at work.

Eating Tip:

You can add other toppings to the burrito bowls if you would like, such as homemade guacamole, lettuce, black beans, and so on. Just make sure they're whole foods!

Nutritional info (1 bowl per serving):
Calories: 903
Protein: 69
Carbs: 31
Fat: 55
Fiber: 3

Tomato and Roasted Red Pepper Soup

Serves: 2
Time: 15 minutes

Soup and half a sandwich is a classic lunch combo. For the soup side, try this rich-tasting tomato and roasted red pepper recipe that's done in about 15 minutes. You can make it the night before or even the morning of, if you have time.

Ingredients:
1-2 cups organic, free-range chicken broth
2 28-ounce cans of chopped tomatoes
1 12-ounce jar of drained roasted red peppers
2 chopped garlic cloves
1 chopped onion
1 handful chopped fresh basil
1 tablespoon olive oil
¼ teaspoon red chili flakes
Sea salt and pepper to taste

Directions:
1. In a soup pot, sauté the onions in olive oil until they become soft.
2. Add the garlic and keep cooking for about 2 minutes.
3. Add the tomatoes and peppers and simmer for 10 minutes.
4. Next, pour in the chicken stock, basil, and chili flakes and simmer a little longer.
5. Using a hand blender or regular blender, puree the soup until completely smooth.

6. Store in a plastic container in the fridge until you're ready to eat.
7. Season to taste with sea salt and pepper if necessary.

Nutritional info (½ total soup per serving):
Calories: 311
Protein: 10
Carbs: 48
Fat: 8
Fiber: 3

Salmon Cakes w/ Cilantro-Lime Avocado Dip
Serves: 8
Time: 15 minutes

These salmon cakes are a great way to get more fish into your diet. They're held together by coconut flour and full-fat coconut milk, and perfectly seasoned with onion, parsley, garlic, dill, and lemon zest. The cakes are bright, flaky, and delicious with a side salad at lunchtime.

Ingredients:
6-ounces of drained, canned salmon
¼ an avocado
1 minced garlic clove
2 tablespoons finely-diced red onion
2 tablespoons coconut oil
1 tablespoon finely-chopped parsley
1 tablespoon diced celery
1 tablespoon coconut flour
½ - 1 tablespoon canned full-fat coconut milk
½ teaspoon dried dill
¼ teaspoon lemon zest
¼ teaspoon sea salt
Black pepper to taste

Buying Tip:

Wild Planet sells wild-caught pink and sockeye salmon. They are available online or in some health food stores.

The rest of the avocado from above

2-3 tablespoons olive oil
1-2 tablespoons water
2 tablespoons minced cilantro
1 tablespoon lime juice
1/2 teaspoon minced garlic
Sea salt to taste

Directions:
1. Begin by making the salmon cakes.
2. Chop the garlic, parsley, onion, and celery.
3. Smash ¼ of an avocado and add in the vegetables from above, including the spices, coconut flour, and salmon.
4. Mix gently with your hands until combined.
5. Add in ½ tablespoon coconut milk and mix. If you need more, add the other ½ tablespoon.
6. Form 14 small patties and store on a plate in the fridge for 30 minutes.
7. Bake in a 400-degree oven for 8-12 minutes, or until the cakes are golden-brown.
8. To make the avocado dip, blend all the ingredients (except olive oil) from the second ingredient list until smooth.
9. Slowly pour in the olive oil while pulsing the processor until you get the texture you want.
10. If it's too thick, add some water.
11. Dollop the dip unto your salmon cakes and enjoy!

Nutritional info (2 cakes per serving w/ avocado dip):
Calories: 135
Protein: 5
Carbs: 3
Fat: 13
Fiber: 3

Chipotle-Lime Chicken Kabobs
Serves: 4-5
Time: 40-45 minutes

Kabobs are one of my favorite summer foods. They're so versatile and almost everything becomes that much more delicious when it's grilled. For these kabobs, you marinate bite-sized chicken chunks in minced chipotles, lime juice, and raw honey, and then stick them on a skewer with red onion, red peppers, and pineapple to be grilled.

This is the perfect leftover food and is just waiting to be taken to work for a tasty lunch that's good warmed up or cold.

Ingredients:
1 pound cut-up boneless chicken breasts
1 cut-up red onion
1 pound cubed fresh pineapple
1-2 cut-up red bell peppers
¼ cup olive oil
¼ cup fresh lime juice
2 minced garlic cloves
2 tablespoons raw honey
2-3 teaspoons of adobo sauce
1 teaspoon minced chipotle chilies
1 teaspoon paprika
Sea salt and pepper to taste

Directions:
1. Whisk the marinade ingredients (olive oil, lime juice, minced garlic, honey, adobo sauce, and chilies) in a bowl.
2. Set half aside for a baste.
3. Season the cut-up chicken with salt, paprika, and pepper before tossing the chicken in the marinade and refrigerating for a half hour.
4. Prepare the pineapple, onion, and red pepper for the skewers.
5. Preheat your grill to medium-high.
6. Stick the chicken and veggies on skewers.
7. Grill for 10-12 minutes, basting with the unused half of the marinade as you go.
8. Serve hot with a side of your choice, like brown rice.

Nutritional info (2 skewers per serving):
Calories: 265
Protein: 22
Carbs: 19
Fat: 12
Fiber: 2

Apple Tuna Salad Lettuce Boats
Serves: 1
Time: 5-7 minutes

This is a great lunch option for people who are really on the go. It takes almost no time to put together in the morning, and there's no microwaving or prep needed to start eating it come noonish. It's on the lighter side of a lunch, so plan on having a snack between this meal and dinner, especially if you have long work days.

Ingredients:
4 romaine lettuce leaves
1 medium-sized apple
1 5-ounce drained can of tuna
1 tablespoon homemade mayo
2 thinly-sliced chives
½ teaspoon Dijon mustard
Black pepper
A sprinkle of lemon juice

Directions:
1. Core the apple and slice it in half.
2. Chop one half in ¼-inch cubes.
3. Mix the apple cubes with the tuna, mustard, mayo, chives, and a squirt of lemon juice to keep the cubes from browning.
4. Bag the lettuce leaves and tuna salad separately.
5. When you're ready to eat, cut the other apple half into 4 wedges, and spoon the tuna salad unto the lettuce leaves along with 1 wedge per leaf.

Nutritional info (whole recipe per serving):
Calories: 278
Protein: 23
Carbs: 24
Fat: 19
Fiber: 4.1

Spaghetti Squash Pasta w/ Grilled Chicken and Basil Avocado Sauce
Serves: 3-4
Time: 40-50 minutes (w/ precooked chicken)

Pasta is probably one of the most missed foods when you're on a whole foods diet, though you can eat certain kinds, but not very often. Spaghetti squash instead of pasta is a genius substitution, and when you add grilled chicken and a basil avocado sauce, you won't miss regular pasta at all. For time's sake, it's best to have already cooked the chicken.

Ingredients:
2-3 cups cooked spaghetti squash
½-1 cup chopped grilled chicken
1 pitted avocado, large
2 tablespoons extra virgin olive oil
1-2 tablespoons fresh lemon juice
1-2 crushed garlic cloves
Sea salt and pepper to taste

Directions:
1. To cook, the squash, preheat the oven to 375-degrees.
2. Cut the squash in half lengthwise and scoop out the seeds.
3. Brush the cut sides with olive oil, sea salt, and pepper.
4. Put the squash cut-side down on a baking tray and bake for 35-45 minutes until you can easily pierce the flesh with a fork.
5. Scrape the flesh out with a fork, it will look like spaghetti strands.
6. To make the sauce, process the avocado, lemon juice, olive oil, basil, and garlic in a food processor until smooth.
7. Add a little salt and pepper.
8. Put the spaghetti strands in a saucepan (low-heat) and pour the sauce over the pasta.
9. If the sauce is too thick, add some water.
10. Stir in the cooked chicken and cook until it's all heated through.
11. For leftovers, just store everything together in the fridge, and microwave when you're ready to eat.

Nutritional info (¼ recipe per serving):
Calories: 224
Protein: 2
Carbs: 10
Fat: 14
Fiber: 5

Creamy Chicken Curry
Serves: 3-4
Time: 40 minutes

This chicken curry keeps really well, so you can have it for a few days' worth of lunch. It has tender chicken, coconut milk, ginger, and other awesome flavors that will energize you for the last half of your day, whether you're at home or at the office.

Ingredients:
1 pound of cut skinless, boneless chicken breasts
¼ cup organic chicken broth
2 chopped medium-sized tomatoes
2 minced garlic cloves
1 tablespoon curry powder
1 can coconut milk
1 sliced medium-sized onion
1 tablespoon grass-fed butter
1 teaspoon grated fresh ginger
1 teaspoon sea salt
¼ teaspoon black pepper

Directions:
1. Season the cut chicken with salt, pepper, and curry.
2. In a skillet, melt the butter and sauté the onion for 3-4 minutes.
3. Add the seasoned chicken, ginger, and garlic and continue to cook until the chicken is almost done.
4. Add the tomatoes and chicken stock.
5. Bring the skillet to a boil before reducing and simmering for 15 minutes without a lid.
6. Next, add the coconut milk and bring to a boil again.
7. Reduce the heat and simmer for 20 minutes, occasionally stirring.
8. Taste and add any more seasonings if necessary before eating.
9. Serving options include cauliflower rice, shredded carrots, and a squeeze of lime.

Nutritional info (¼ recipe per serving, just the chicken curry):
Calories: 297
Protein: 37
Carbs: 6
Fat: 13
Fiber: 4

Turkey Avocado Wraps

Serves: 1-2
Time: Less than 5 minutes

I know I've said that such-and-such recipe was the fastest lunch ever, but *this* may truly be the quickest option for busy people looking for something healthy and filling. With just three ingredients and a homemade vinaigrette of your choice, you have a tasty, low-calorie meal.

Ingredients:
4 deli turkey slices
8 very small avocado slices
Two handfuls of shredded carrots
A drizzle of whole-food approved vinaigrette

Directions:
1. Lay out two turkey slices on top of each other. This is your "bread."
2. Arrange some shredded carrots on top, followed by a few avocado slices.
3. Drizzle on a little vinaigrette and roll the wrap.
4. Repeat for another wrap.
5. Enjoy!

Nutritional info (2 wraps/1 whole recipe per serving):
Calories: 481
Protein: 44
Carbs: 26
Fat: 22
Fiber: 7

Paleo Pad Thai
Serves: 4
Time: About an hour (40 minutes less if using precooked spaghetti squash)

Pad Thai is traditionally made with rice noodles and is a staple of Thailand street food and casual cafes. This version uses spaghetti squash, along with an awesome almond-butter based sauce that uses coconut milk, ginger, and lime for creaminess and flavor.

Ingredients:
1 pound cut chicken

½ medium-sized spaghetti squash
3 chopped cups of carrots, broccoli, zucchini
2 whisked eggs
2-3 minced garlic cloves
½ cup homemade chicken broth
½ cup canned coconut milk
½ cup almond butter
Juice from one large lime
2 tablespoons toasted sesame oil
1 tablespoon coconut aminos
1 tablespoon apple cider vinegar
1 tablespoon fresh grated ginger
¼ teaspoon sea salt
⅛ teaspoon cayenne pepper
Coconut oil (for cooking)

Directions:
1. If you don't have pre-cooked spaghetti squash, cook it first.
2. Cut the spaghetti squash in half and scoop out the seeds.
3. Season with salt, pepper, and olive oil.
4. Place on a baking tray, cut-side down, and bake for 40-45 minutes until fork-tender in a 375-degree oven.
5. Scrape the flesh out with a fork and set aside for now.
6. To make the sauce, mix all the ingredients in the second ingredient list (beginning with ½ cup homemade broth) and stir over low-heat.
7. In a separate skillet, heat 1 tablespoon coconut oil and brown the cut-up chicken.
8. Add the garlic and sauté for the last minute or so.
9. Remove the chicken and garlic from the skillet.
10. Add some more oil and pour in the eggs.
11. Cook until done and remove from the skillet.
12. In the same skillet, sauté the veggies for 4-5 minutes.
13. Add the chicken, cooked eggs, and sauce to this skillet and mix.
14. Add the spaghetti squash and mix again to heat up.
15. Serve with cilantro, lime wedges, or other favorite Pad Thai toppings.

Nutritional info (¼ whole Pad Thai recipe):
Calories: 617
Protein: 37
Carbs: 29

Fat: 42
Fiber: 3.7

Spicy-Lime Salmon
Serves: 1-2 servings
Time: 20 minutes

Salmon and lime together is one of my favorite flavor combinations. The acidity of the lime really brightens up the rich fattiness of the fish, and this recipe adds a little heat to the party with chopped jalapenos. You can eat this salmon as is, or with a side like brown rice or salad.

Ingredients:
1-2 pound salmon fillet
2 tablespoons flat-leaf parsley
2 tablespoons olive oil
1 garlic clove
1 zested and juiced lime
½ seeded and chopped jalapeno

Directions:
1. Preheat your oven to 400-degrees.
2. Rinse the salmon and pat dry with a paper towel.
3. Line a baking sheet with foil and put the fish on top.
4. In a food processor, mix the lime zest, lime juice, parsley, garlic, olive oil, and jalapeno.
5. Pour this sauce over the salmon.
6. Bake for 18-20 minutes.

Nutritional info (½ of recipe per serving):
Calories: 327
Protein: 46
Carbs: 24
Fat: 25
Fiber: 0

Grilled Chicken w/ Strawberry Salsa
Serves: 4
Time: 1 hour, 5 minutes

This recipe is the perfect summer meal: it combines grilling, the ideal summer cooking method, with fresh ingredients like strawberries and avocado. It's a simple dish, but it's not simple on flavor.

Ingredients:
4 boneless, skinless chicken breasts
1 juiced lime
2 tablespoons olive oil
2 tablespoons chopped cilantro
1 teaspoon chili powder
¾ teaspoon cumin
¾ teaspoon sea salt
½ teaspoon black pepper
1 cup chopped fresh strawberries
1 diced avocado
1 juiced lime
2 tablespoons finely-chopped red onion
2 tablespoons minced cilantro
½ teaspoon minced, seeded jalapeno
¼ teaspoon sea salt

Directions:
1. Mix the dry marinade ingredients together (cumin, chili powder, salt, pepper) and season both sides of the chicken breasts.
2. In another bowl, mix the lime juice, garlic, cilantro, and olive oil.
3. Put the chicken in the bag and marinate for at least an hour in the fridge.
4. To make the salsa, just mix all the ingredients in the second list and store in the fridge.
5. Grill the chicken over medium-high heat for 5 minutes (per side) until done.
6. Let the meat rest before cutting.
7. Serve with the salsa.

Nutritional info (1 chicken breast + ¼ of strawberry salsa per serving):
Calories: 192
Protein: 11
Carbs: 7
Fat: 14
Fiber: 1

Chicken-Mushroom Bites

Serves: 8
Time: 55 minutes

These mini egg muffins can really be eaten any time of day, but I've included them in the lunch section of the book because they embody so many lunchtime necessities: easy, nutritious, and portable.

Ingredients:
5 organic eggs
½ pound mushrooms
1 cup shredded cooked chicken
⅓ cup coconut milk
2 onions
2 tablespoons ghee
¼ teaspoon salt
¼ teaspoon black pepper
Coconut oil

Eating Tip:

"Ghee" is a form of clarified butter that is used frequently in Indian and South Asian cooking. You can find it at ethnic markets or anywhere Indian food and spices are sold.

Directions:
1. Preheat the oven to 350-degrees and grease a 24-cup mini muffin tin with coconut oil.
2. In a skillet, melt the ghee.
3. Cut the onions into thin slices and cook about 20 minutes, or until the onions are soft and brown.
4. Move to a mixing cool.
5. In the food processor, dice the mushrooms very finely and cook in the skillet for 15 minutes.
6. Add to the onion bowl.
7. Once cool, pour in the coconut milk, chicken, salt, and pepper.
8. Whisk in the eggs and then pour into the muffin tin.
9. Cook for about 15 minutes until the eggs have set.
10. Cool for 10 minutes before eating.

Nutritional info (3 bites per serving):
Calories: 124
Protein: 10
Carbs: 5
Fat: 7
Fiber: 1

Italian Sausage-Potato Skillet
Serves: 5
Time: About 10 minutes

This hearty lunch uses pre-cooked Italian sausage, which cuts down on the cooking time. The rest of the skillet is packed with veggies like bell peppers, potatoes, and zucchini, and it's all seasoned with homemade Italian seasoning. It heats up really well for a Tupperware lunch, and doesn't need any accompaniments.

Ingredients:
1 pound of pre-cooked Italian sausage
1 diced red bell pepper
1 diced green bell pepper
2 peeled, small white sweet potatoes, sliced into circles
1 zucchini sliced into circles
½ diced onion
1 teaspoon oregano
1 teaspoon basil
1 teaspoon parsley
½ teaspoon garlic powder
¼ teaspoon red pepper flakes
Sea salt and pepper to taste

Directions:
1. Combine the last six ingredients in a bowl and set aside.
2. Heat some coconut oil in a skillet and brown the pre-cooked sausage.
3. Remove and plate.
4. In the same skillet, add a little more oil and the potato slices.
5. Spread them out and brown them on one side.
6. Add the peppers, zucchini, onions, and seasoning from the first step on top of the potatoes.
7. Cook for 5 minutes.
8. Push the veggies aside and turn over the potatoes, so they cook on the other side for 5 minutes.

9.   Add any salt and pepper if necessary.
10. Put the sausages in the pan with the veggies until everything is heated through.
11. Eat and enjoy!

Nutritional info (⅕ the skillet per serving):
Calories: 418
Protein: 15
Carbs: 17
Fat: 32
Fiber: 3

Sweet Potato Sloppy Joe's

Serves: 4
Time: 20 minutes

If you have a bunch of baked sweet potatoes, and don't know what to do with them, this is a great recipe. Instead of using hamburger for sloppy joe's, use the potatoes! They add a nice sweetness that cuts the acid of the tomatoes and peppers.

Ingredients:
4 baked sweet potatoes
14-ounces of diced tomatoes
6-ounces of tomato paste
1 ½ pounds of grass-fed ground beef
½ diced green bell pepper
½ diced red bell pepper
½ diced onion
¼ cup diced celery
1 minced garlic clove
2 tablespoons honey
1 tablespoon chili powder
1 teaspoon cumin

Directions:
1.   Sauté the celery, garlic, and onions until the onions become tender.
2.   Add the ground beef and brown.
3.   When brown, add the honey, bell peppers, and dry spices.
4.   Pour in the diced tomatoes (with the liquid) and tomato paste.
5.   Simmer for 15 minutes.

6. Season to taste with salt and pepper.
7. To serve, cut the sweet potatoes in half and scoop out a little bowl for the sloppy joe mixture.

<u>Nutritional info (1 sweet potato w/ sloppy joe mix per serving):</u>
Calories: 586
Protein: 39
Carbs: 60
Fat: 22
Fiber: 3.9

Chicken Tostadas w/ Cauliflower Tortillas
Serves: 6
Time: 45 minutes-50 minutes

This isn't the quickest lunch in terms of initial prep, but once it's done, it makes fantastic leftovers, *and* you get to eat tortillas! They're homemade and made with cauliflower. The chicken mixture is full of peppers, honey, and lime, and finished off with a creamy avocado sauce.

<u>Ingredients:</u>
2-3 cups cooked shredded chicken
5-6 tomatillos
3 garlic cloves
½ cup leaves-only chopped cilantro
2 chopped and seeded Poblano peppers
1 chopped and seeded jalapeno
2 Anaheim chopped and seeded peppers
1 small chopped onion
1 lime
1-2 tablespoons honey
Olive oil
Salt and pepper to taste
¾ head of "riced" cauliflower (cauliflower put through a food processor to resemble rice grains)
2 eggs
Sea salt and pepper to taste
2 pitted and chopped avocados
Juice of 1 lime
Juice of 1 lemon
½ cup chopped cilantro (leaves only again)
½ teaspoon garlic

<u>Directions:</u>

1. Preheat the oven to 350-degrees and line a cookie sheet with foil.
2. Put the chopped onion, peppers, and garlic on the cookie sheet before drizzling with olive oil, salt, and pepper.
3. Roast for 20 minutes.
4. Puree the roasted veggies.
5. Add the juice from one lime, a tablespoon of honey, and cilantro.
6. Taste and add water if you want a smoother sauce.
7. Time for the tortillas.
8. Preheat the oven to 375-degrees and prepare a baking tray with parchment paper.
9. Process the cauliflower until you get 2 cups of packed rice.
10. Microwave for 2 minutes and stir, then microwave again for another 2 minutes and stir.
11. Squeeze the rice in a dish towel to get rid of excess water.
12. Add a few tablespoons of the green chili sauce you made before adding the two eggs, pepper, and salt.
13. Stir.
14. It will be a bit runny, but it shouldn't be a liquid.
15. Spread the mixture into 6 small flat circles, the size of small tortillas.
16. Bake for 10 minutes and carefully peel off the parchment.
17. Flip and bake for another 5-7 minutes.
18. When they're done, heat a medium-sized pan and press the tortillas down to crisp them up.
19. For the avocado sauce, processor 2 chopped avocados, the juice of 1 lemon and 1 lime, and garlic.
20. Add ½ cup chopped cilantro.
21. Mix the chili sauce with the cooked shredded chicken and place a healthy amount on top of a tortilla.
22. Finish off with a dollop of the avocado sauce, and serve!

<u>Nutritional info (1 chicken tostada w/ avocado sauce):</u>
Calories: 278
Protein: 28
Carbs: 22
Fat: 9
Fiber: 1.5

Avocado-Shrimp Boats

Serves: 4
Time: 10 minutes or less

If you have a grill and like to experiment with different foods, you'll love this recipe. Using just an avocado, some shrimp, a few veggies, and seasonings, you can make a unique, delicious lunch that serves as it's own bowl. This recipe makes four avocado halves stuffed with a shrimp salsa, that's all livened up with flavors like onion, paprika, lime, and hot sauce.

Ingredients:
2 avocados
20 medium, raw peeled shrimp
1 chopped and seeded tomato
¼ cup diced red onion
1 diced jalapeno
3 tablespoons chopped cilantro, leaves only
2 tablespoons olive oil
1 tablespoon hot sauce
Juice of 2 limes
1 ½ teaspoons paprika
1 teaspoon sea salt
1 teaspoon cayenne
½ teaspoon garlic powder
½ teaspoon onion powder
½ teaspoon thyme
½ teaspoon basil

Directions:
1. Cut the avocados in half lengthwise and take out the pits.
2. Squeeze one lime on the cut avocado and brush with 1 tablespoon olive oil.
3. In a bowl, squeeze out the rest of the lime juice and add 1 tablespoon of olive oil before mixing in onion, tomato, cilantro, hot sauce, and salt and pepper.
4. Preheat the grill to medium-high.
5. In another bowl, mix the shrimp seasoning (paprika, cayenne, salt, garlic, onion, thyme, pepper, and basil)
6. Cook the shrimp on skewers and sprinkle liberally with the seasoning.
7. Grill the avocados for a few minutes until grill marks appear.
8. The shrimp should take about 3 minutes each side.

·om the grill, carefully pull off from the skewers,

the shrimp with the salsa and spoon into each
alf. You should get about 4-5 shrimp per half.

Nutritional info (1 avocado half w/ shrimp salsa):
Calories: 567
Protein: 92
Carbs: 13
Fat: 22
Fiber: 9

Zesty Chicken Nuggets
Serves: 3
Time: 35 minutes

You probably remember chicken nuggets from your childhood. They were usually all-white meat encased in breading, that were high in salt and fat. This recipe makes things all-natural, and even though they aren't shaped like dinosaurs, they're good enough for your kids to forgive that fact.

Ingredients:
1 pound of organic, boneless chicken breasts
1 egg
½ cup almond meal
1 teaspoon Italian seasoning
½ teaspoon garlic powder
¼ teaspoon water
¼ teaspoon paprika
¼ teaspoon cayenne pepper
¼ teaspoon sea salt
¼ teaspoon red pepper flakes
¼ teaspoon chili powder

Directions:
1. Preheat the oven to 400-degrees and line a baking sheet with tin foil.
2. Grease the foil with a little olive oil.
3. In a bowl, mix all the spices and almond meal.
4. In a separate bowl, break the egg along with ¼ teaspoon of water and whisk together.

5. Cut the chicken into small, bite-sized pieces.
6. Coat the chicken in the egg before rolling in the spice/flour mixture.
7. Arrange on the greased foil and bake for 12-15 minutes.
8. Flip and cook for another 10-12 minutes until crispy.
9. Serve right away with a homemade, whole-food approved dipping sauce.

Nutritional info (⅓ of the chicken nuggets):
Calories: 300
Protein: 36
Carbs: 4
Fat: 16
Fiber: 0

Creole Pork 'n Rice
Serves: 2-4
Time: 50 minutes

This take on pork and rice has you substitute white rice for a much healthier cauliflower rice. It's flavored with melted coconut oil full of herbs and spices, giving the whole dish a little Creole flare. The recipe makes enough pork 'n rice for two very hungry people, or four people looking for a lighter lunch portion.

Ingredients:
2 heads fresh cauliflower
1 pound cooked cubed pork chops
½ cup red bell pepper
½ cup green bell pepper
½ cup diced onion
3 minced garlic cloves
2-3 tablespoons melted coconut oil
½ tablespoon dried thyme leaves
1 teaspoon black pepper
1 teaspoon sea salt
½ teaspoon ground cayenne pepper
¼ teaspoon celery seed

Directions:
1. Preheat the oven to 425-degrees
2. Break the cauliflower into florets and cut off the stems.
3. Process the cauliflower to a rice-like texture.

4. Put the rice in a large mixing bowl and add the pork cubes, onion, and bell peppers, and mix.
5. In a separate bowl, mix the melted coconut oil, thyme, garlic, salt, cayenne, celery seed, and black pepper.
6. Pour over the cauliflower rice and toss so everything is coated.
7. Take out two rimmed baking sheets and divide up the rice between them.
8. Roast for 30-35 minutes, stirring at the 15-minute mark so it doesn't burn.
9. The rice is done when it is tender and a little brown.

Nutritional info (½ of the pork rice for a heartier lunch)
Calories: 626
Protein: 56
Carbs: 35
Fat: 39
Fiber: 12

Turkish Stuffed Eggplant
Serves: 4
Time: 1 hour, 15 minutes

Eggplant doesn't appear in a ton of dishes, and lots of people complain about a bitter taste. However, thanks to the half-hour soak, these beef-stuffed eggplants are tender and spicy with flavors like green chilies and garlic. A great alternative to stuffed zucchini or squash.

Ingredients:
2 large eggplants, cut in half lengthwise
1 pound grass-fed, organic ground beef
4 long jalapeno chilies
2 minced garlic cloves
2 medium-sized tomatoes, one sliced into 4 slices, the other chopped
1 diced onion
1 chopped handful of fresh parsley
2 tablespoons coconut oil
1 tablespoon tomato paste
2 teaspoons sea salt
½ teaspoon salt and pepper

Directions:
1. Slice the eggplants in half lengthwise.
2. Put the eggplants in a bowl of water with 2 teaspoons of salt, so they are submerged.
3. Weigh them down somehow (or else they will float), so they are completely underwater.
4. Soak them for 30 minutes.
5. In the meantime, heat a skillet and cook the beef for about 4 minutes, or until most of the pinkness is gone.
6. Sauté the onions with the meat until the onions become soft.
7. Add the tomatoes (leaving out the four slices), garlic, tomato paste, salt, and pepper.
8. Simmer for 5 minutes.
9. Toss in the chopped parsley and any more seasoning if necessary.
10. Take out the eggplants, rinse well, and then dry.
11. Sprinkle them with salt and pepper.
12. Heat 2 tablespoons of coconut oil in a skillet and put in the eggplant cut-side down to brown.
13. It should take about 4 minutes, and once brown, move to a paper towel.
14. Preheat the oven to 400-degrees.
15. With a spoon, scoop out the eggplant seeds to make a little channel for the filling.
16. Fill and then top with half of a chili pepper and a tomato slice.
17. Bake the eggplants for 20-30 minutes.
18. Before eating, wait for a few minutes.

Nutritional info (1 stuffed eggplant half per serving)
Calories: 486
Protein: 23
Carbs: 24
Fat: 34
Fiber: 3.4

Zucchini Noodles w/ Quick Pesto
Serves: 4
Time: 5-7 minutes

This is another great noodle substitute lunch, this time using zucchini for pasta and pre-grilled chicken. It comes together really quickly, with the pesto ingredients making about 1 cup of pesto. If you need more, just double or triple the items.

Ingredients:
2 big, grilled chicken breasts
5 zucchinis sliced into noodles
2 cups basil leaves
½ cup olive oil
2-ounces pine nuts
1 tablespoon lemon juice
1 garlic clove
1 teaspoon olive oil
Salt and pepper to taste

Directions:
1. Mix the pesto ingredients (2 cups of basil - 1 garlic clove) in a food processor until coarsely-combined.
2. Shred the zucchini into noodles and sauté in a pan with a teaspoon of olive oil until tender. This should only take a few minutes.
3. Mix the pesto sauce in with the noodles.
4. Add the pre-cooked chicken and mix until everything is heated through.
5. Serve!

Nutritional info (¼ noodles and pesto recipe)
Calories: 411
Protein: 15
Carbs: 13
Fat: 36
Fiber: 4

Creamy Asparagus Soup
Serves: 4-6
Time: 40 minutes

This soup is velvety with a gentle, fresh taste, but unlike a lot of cream of asparagus soups, it isn't too rich, thanks to the inclusion of plain Greek yogurt instead of cream. Pureed asparagus and chicken stock make a great base, and the asparagus is chock-full of nutrients like fiber, vitamin K, and antioxidants. Organic bacon and a few pinches of cayenne pepper add a little more complexity to the soup.

Ingredients:
6 cups chicken broth
2 pounds asparagus
14 ounces of white beans, drained
3-4 slices of chopped, grass-fed organic bacon
⅓ cup plain Greek yogurt
1 chopped onion
2 tablespoons grass-fed butter
1 lemon
1-3 pinches of cayenne pepper

Directions:
1. Sauté the onions in the butter for 2-3 minutes.
2. Cut the tops off the asparagus and set asides. Chop off the woody ends, as well.
3. Chop the asparagus into short bits and add to the onion pot. Sauté for 3-5 minutes.
4. The asparagus will be bright and tender. Add the beans, cayenne, and stock.
5. Simmer uncovered for 20 minutes.
6. With an immersion blender or regular blender, puree until smooth.
7. Spoon in the yogurt and puree again.
8. Season with salt and pepper, and a squeeze from the lemon.
9. In a separate skillet, brown the bacon.
10. Next, add the asparagus tops and sauté it all together for 1-2 minutes.
11. Garnish the soup with the chopped bacon and asparagus tops.

Nutritional info (about 1 cup per serving)
Calories: 263
Protein: 18
Carbs: 4
Fat: 37
Fiber: 4

Easy Zucchini and Smoked Salmon Roll-Ups
Serves: 2
Time: 10 minutes

Sliced zucchini makes a great vehicle for roll-ups, and this one with smoked salmon is delicious. You only need five ingredients to bring out the natural flavors of the squash and fish. If you don't like smoked salmon, you can substitute for another whole-food approved deli meat, though it probably won't have that buttery saltiness that smoked salmon is known for.

Ingredients:
1 medium-sized washed and dried zucchini
4 slices of smoked salmon
Salt
Pepper
Olive oil

Directions:
1. First, set your oven to broil and prepare a baking sheet with foil greased in olive oil.
2. Slice the zucchini lengthwise. It should be thin enough so when they are cooked, you can roll them up. Think about ¼ an inch.
3. Lay the zucchini on the baking sheet and season with olive oil, sea salt, and pepper.
4. Broil for 3 minutes before turning them over, and seasoning again.
5. Finish off at 2-4 minutes until they are tender.
6. Cut your smoked salmon so they are the same length and width as your zucchini.
7. Roll the smoked salmon inside the zucchini and secure with a toothpick.
8. Serve with a small serving of brown rice with fresh fruit for dessert, and you have a healthy lunch ready to go!

Nutritional info (2 roll-ups per serving)
Calories: 293
Protein: 24
Carbs: 11
Fat: 17
Fiber: 2

Simple Crispy Chicken
Serves: 2
Time: About 25 minutes

You need a good basic chicken recipe in your repertoire. This one guarantees you get a beautifully-crispy skin, so the chicken is the true star of lunchtime, not just a necessary protein filler. With chicken this good, it really doesn't matter what sides you choose.

Ingredients:
8 bone in, skin-on chicken thighs
1 tablespoon sea salt
2 teaspoons grass-fed butter
Black pepper to taste
Garlic powder to taste

Directions:
1. Using a *sharp* pair of kitchen shears, cut out the bone carefully around the cartilage and joint, so you lose as little meat as possible.
2. Flatten the chicken with a mallet. This will allow the meat to cook evenly.
3. With the skin-side facing up, season evenly with salt.

Cooking Tip:

You can season evenly by sprinkling salt with your hands raised high, imitating falling raindrops.

4. Heat a cast-iron skillet and melt the butter.
5. Lay down the chicken thighs (four will probably fit) with the skin facing down.
6. Season with pepper and garlic powder to taste. You can add any other seasonings if you like. I'm a fan of keeping it simple with salt, pepper, and garlic.
7. Leave the chicken alone so the skin can fry, for about 7-10 minutes. Rotate the pan 90-degrees around 4 minutes in so the heat is even.
8. Flip the chicken and cook for 3 minutes until it reaches 165-degrees internally.
9. Move the chicken to a wire rack while you finish the rest of the thighs.
10. Wait 5 minutes before cutting into the freshly-cooked chicken.

Nutritional info (4 wings per serving)
Calories: 697
Protein: 76

Carbs: 0
Fat: 20
Fiber: 0

Asian Lettuce Wrap
Serves: 4
Time: 20 minutes

We've done quite a few wraps, but honestly, you could eat wraps every day of the week and prepare them slightly differently, and you would never get sick of them. This recipe is for an Asian turkey lettuce wrap with fresh ginger and a crunchy cabbage-carrot slaw.

Ingredients:
1 pound ground turkey
3 minced garlic cloves
4 cups shredded carrots + cabbage
2 cups chopped mushrooms
1 diced onion
1 chopped bell pepper
¼ cup coconut aminos
1 tablespoon olive oil
1 teaspoon fresh ginger
1 teaspoon ground mustard
Salt and pepper to taste
Butter lettuce

Directions:
1. Brown the turkey in a skillet with a tablespoon of olive oil.
2. When the meat is cooked, add the veggies, including the garlic, and spices.
3. Sauté for 10-15 minutes until everything is tender and mixed.
4. Lay out the lettuce leaves and spoon on a healthy amount of the meat mixture.
5. Optional garnishes include cashews, chives, cilantro, and so on.

Nutritional info (1 wrap per serving)
Calories: 290
Protein: 26
Carbs: 19
Fat: 13
Fiber: 3

Portabella Sandwich

Serves: 2
Time: 20 minutes

Instead of bread, this creative sandwich uses portabella mushrooms, which contain the Big Three - fat, carbs, and protein. Other sandwich ingredients include juicy chicken cutlets, turkey bacon, fresh tomato and spinach, and guacamole.

Ingredients:
4 portabella caps
1 cooked boneless, skinless chicken cutlet cut into two pieces
½ cup fresh spinach leaves
2 slices of fresh tomato
2 slices cooked turkey bacon
3 tablespoons guacamole
2 tablespoons coconut oil

Directions:
1. Prepare the mushrooms by removing the stem and scooping out the gills.
2. In a skillet, cook the mushrooms in a little coconut oil for 3-5 minutes on each side.
3. Remove the mushrooms and assemble the sandwich.
4. First put on one chicken cutlet, turkey bacon, spinach, tomato, and 1 ½ tablespoons of the guacamole. Put on another mushroom cap.
5. Repeat to make a total of 2 sandwiches.

Nutritional info (1 stack per serving)
Calories: 392
Protein: 26
Carbs: 19
Fat: 25
Fiber: 4

Chapter 10 - Dinner

Bun-less Caramelized Onion Burgers w/ Avocado
Serves: 6
Time: About 30 minutes

Who doesn't love burgers for dinner, especially when they're homemade? These surprisingly simple burgers use lean ground beef to make quarter-pounders, with onions caramelized in balsamic vinegar. It's all topped off with beefsteak tomatoes and avocados. Everyone will feel full and happy, without any of the guilt usually associated with fast-food burgers.

Ingredients:
1 ½ pounds of lean, grass-fed ground beef
3 avocados
2 thinly-sliced onions
1 beefsteak tomato
2 tablespoons balsamic vinegar
2 tablespoons coconut oil
1 teaspoon garlic powder
1 teaspoon sea salt
1 teaspoon fresh black pepper

Directions:
1. Heat 1 tablespoon of coconut oil and then add the sliced onions.
2. Sauté for 10-15 minutes, stirring every once and awhile.
3. Pour in the balsamic vinegar and continue to sauté for 5 minutes.
4. Set the onions aside.
5. With your hands, form six patties with the meat.
6. Sprinkle both sides with pepper, garlic powder, and salt.
7. Heat a skillet with 1 tablespoon of coconut oil.
8. Sauté the burgers for 3-5 minutes on each side, for a total of 6-10 minutes.
9. Remove from heat and let the meat rest for 1 minute.
10. Cut the tomato into 6 slices and pit and slice the avocados.

11. Place a burger on top of a tomato slice, followed by 2 tablespoons of the caramelized onions, and topped with avocado.
12. Serve with homemade ketchup and mustard if desired.

Nutritional info (1 burger per serving)
Calories: 657
Protein: 42
Carbs: 19
Fat: 41
Fiber: 1

Chicken + Bacon Sweet Potato Boats
Serve: 4
Time: 30 minutes

Sweet potatoes make great edible bowls. They're packed with nutrients like vitamin A and Vitamin C, and mild enough to compliment other flavors, like onion, bacon, thyme, and mushrooms. This is a great recipe if you have some baked sweet potatoes and chicken, and aren't sure what to do.

Ingredients:
2 large baked sweet potatoes
2-3 cups shredded cooked chicken
4 diced slices of bacon
12-ounces of sliced fresh mushrooms
2 minced garlic cloves
2 cups spinach
1 chopped onion
½ teaspoon dried thyme
Salt and pepper to taste
A drizzle of fruity olive oil

Cooking Tip:

Fruity olive oils include Monterosa Verdeal (medium fruity) or Villa Magra (more intense fruitiness), which you can find at places like Whole Foods.

Directions:

1. Cut the sweet potatoes in half, lengthwise, and scoop out the flesh.
2. Dice up the flesh.
3. In a skillet, cook the diced bacon until the fat starts to sizzle, and then add the sweet potato flesh, mushrooms, garlic, onion, shredded chicken, and thyme.
4. Stir frequently until the veggies are tender and the bacon crisps up.
5. Season with salt and pepper.
6. Remove from the heat and add the spinach.
7. Wait to let the spinach wilt.
8. Once wilted, add the skillet contents to the sweet potato boats.
9. Finish off with a drizzle of fruity olive oil and serve!

Nutritional info (1 sweet potato boat w/ filling per serving)
Calories: 363
Protein: 55
Carbs: 15
Fat: 9
Fiber: 4

Meat Lover's Chili
Serves: 6-8
Time: 35 minutes

When the weather is cold and you come in from the snow or freezing rain, a bowl of steaming-hot chili would really hit the spot. This is the chili you should make. It's packed with three kinds of meat (Italian sausage, round steak, and sirloin) and a little red wine for that rich, deep flavor.

Ingredients:
2 pounds ground sirloin
1 pound round steak cut into bite-sized pieces
6-ounces of Italian sausage
8 minced garlic cloves
2 cups chopped yellow onion
1 ½ cups bell pepper
¼ cup red wine
2 28-ounce cans of chopped tomatoes (w/ juice)
2 tablespoons chili powder
2 bay leaves

1 tablespoon ancho chili pepper
1 tablespoon cumin
3 teaspoons tomato paste
1 teaspoon dried oregano

Directions:
1. Begin by removing the casings from the sausage and chopping the bell peppers.
2. Heat a pan and put in all the meat, bell pepper, onion, and garlic.
3. Once the meat is browned, add the tomato paste, chili powder, ancho chili, cumin, oregano, bay leaves, salt, and pepper.
4. Cook for 1 minute while you stir constantly.
5. Add the wine and bring the pan to a boil.
6. When it's starts to boil, reduce the heat and simmer for a half-hour, stirring every now and then.
7. Pick out the bay leaves and serve!

Nutritional info (⅛ chili recipe per serving)
Calories: 435
Protein: 43
Carbs: 11
Fat: 20
Fiber: 0

Dover Sole w/ Homemade Remoulade + Shrimp
Serves: 8
Time: About 40 minutes

This is the kind of gourmet seafood dish you make for the holidays. The remoulade sauce requires three ingredients (mayonnaise, spicy brown mustard, and horseradish) you probably have to make yourself, but if you are committed to the whole-food lifestyle, they are essential condiments that you can use for a large variety of dishes.

Ingredients:
¾ cup homemade mayo
1 ½ tablespoons pickles
1 tablespoon lemon juice
1 tablespoon homemade spicy brown mustard
½ tablespoon homemade horseradish

2 teaspoons chopped fresh parsley
1 teaspoon finely-chopped capers
1 teaspoon dried chives
¼ teaspoon dried leaf tarragon
A drizzle of honey
½ cup Panko bread crumbs
2 tablespoons veggie oil
2 tablespoons minced fresh rosemary
2 minced garlic cloves
1 tablespoon Dijon mustard
Salt and pepper to taste
1 pound peeled and deveined fresh shrimp
8 fresh skinless, sole fillets
8-ounces Greek yogurt
1 tablespoon Dijon mustard
Salt and pepper to taste

Directions:
1. Combine the ingredients in the first list for the remoulade and store in the fridge, so the flavors can deepen.
2. Preheat the oven to 420-degrees.
3. Mince the shrimp and combine with salt, pepper, Greek yogurt, and Dijon.
4. Place the shrimp mixture on top of the sole fillets and roll the fillet, so the fillet becomes stuffed.
5. Secure with a toothpick.
6. Put the stuffed fillets into a greased baking dish and bake for 10 minutes.
7. In the meantime, mix the ingredients in the second list of ingredients.
8. When the fillets have cooked for 10 minutes, remove from oven and top with the Panko mixture.
9. Cook for another 15-20 minutes until the shrimp stuffing has melted and the fish becomes flaky.
10. Serve right away with the remoulade.

Nutritional info (1 stuffed sole w/ sauce and Panko topping per serving)
Calories: 412
Protein: 50
Carbs: 4
Fat: 38
Fiber: 1

Slow Cooker Lemongrass-Coconut Chicken Thighs

Serves: 4
Time: 4-5 hours

I love the flavor of this chicken. The lemongrass is fresh and citrusy-spicy, while the coconut adds a tropical sweetness. After mixing the marinade and slathering the chicken, it's pretty hands off, thanks to the slow cooker.

Ingredients:
10 drumsticks, skin removed
1 thick stalk of fresh lemongrass
4 minced garlic cloves
1 cup coconut milk
¼ cup chopped fresh scallions
1 thinly-sliced onion
3 tablespoons coconut aminos
2 tablespoons Red Boat fish sauce (this brand is whole-food approved)
Thumb of ginger, zested
1 teaspoon five-spice powder
Sea salt
Fresh black pepper

Directions:
1. Remove the papery skins from the lemongrass, remove the bottom, and trim to about 5 inches.
2. Put the lemongrass, ginger, garlic, coconut milk, fish sauce, five-spice powder, and coconut aminos into a blender and puree until smooth.
3. Pour the sauce over the chicken and mix till coated.
4. Put the chopped onion in the bottom of the slow cooker and put the chicken thighs on top.
5. Cook on LOW for 4-5 hours. Do not cook longer than 5 hours.
6. When they're done, serve hot with some chopped scallions as a garnish and a side of your choice, like brown rice.

Nutritional info (2.5 thighs per serving)
Calories: 242
Protein: 29
Carbs: 8

Fat: 10
Fiber: 0

Pork Chops w/ Sautéed Apples
Serves: 2
Time: 30-35 minutes

Pork and apples are a classic combination, and when you follow this recipe, they are just as delicious as you remember. It's also a relatively quick dinner-for-two to put together, and doesn't need any extra side dishes.

<u>Ingredients:</u>
2 bone-in pork chops
½ teaspoon salt
¼ teaspoon coriander
¼ teaspoon nutmeg
¼ teaspoon ground ginger
⅛ cinnamon
⅛ teaspoon cayenne
⅛ teaspoon nutmeg
Butter for cooking
3 cored gala apples
1-2 tablespoons coconut sugar
1 tablespoon grass-fed butter
1 tablespoon water
¾ teaspoon cinnamon
¼ teaspoon nutmeg
⅛ teaspoon allspice

<u>Directions:</u>
1. Take out the pork chops and let them reach room temperature.
2. Pat them dry with a paper towel.
3. Mix the seasonings in the first list and rub on both sides of the pork chops.
4. Preheat the oven to 400-degrees.
5. In a saucepan (which can go in an oven), coat the bottom with butter.
6. Heat until it sizzles and sear the chops for 1-2 minutes.
7. Flip and then transfer right away to the oven.
8. Cook for 3-6 minutes, or until the pork reaches 135-degrees.

9. Plate and let the pork rest for 10 minutes. Do not eat until the temperature reaches 145-degrees.
10. While the meat rests, peel, core, and slice the apples
11. Mix apples with the rest of the ingredients in the second list.
12. Add the butter and water to a pan and heat.
13. Cook the apples for 7-10 minutes in the pan, or until tender.
14. Serve the apples on top of the chops.

Nutritional info (1 pork chop w/ sautéed apple topping per serving)
Calories: 400
Protein: 23
Carbs: 40
Fat: 16
Fiber: 3

Simple 'n Delicious Salmon Burgers
Serves: 4 people
Time: About 10 minutes

This is one of the easiest burger recipes you could hope for. It's a great way to eat salmon that's different than just a fillet, and four burgers only take 10 minutes to grill up. Serve on top of a salad, with mashed sweet potatoes, or any other side you love.

Ingredients:
1 pound salmon fillet
½ cup Panko breadcrumbs
1 slightly beaten egg
½ cup chopped red pepper
½ cup yellow onion
½ teaspoon sea salt
½ teaspoons black pepper
Pinch of chili pepper flakes

Directions:
1. Pull off the salmon skin and mince.
2. Add the salmon and rest of the ingredients into a bowl.
3. Mix with your hands.
4. Mold 4 small patties about ½-inch thick.
5. Heat a grill to medium-high heat.
6. Cook on each side for 4 minutes, for a total of 8 minutes.
7. Serve with homemade tartar sauce (recipe here) and a side of your choice.

Nutritional info (1 salmon burger per serving)
Calories: 300
Protein: 26
Carbs: 8
Fat: 14
Fiber: 1

Spicy Crab California Cones
Serves: 4
Time: 5 minutes

If you're looking for a lighter, quick-fix dinner, these California rolls are awesome. You use cooked lump crab spiced up with red pepper flakes and lime, and wrap it up with some Japanese cucumbers in a seaweed sheet. It's a meal you can hold.

Ingredients:
8 toasted nori sheets, cut in half lengthwise
1 pound cooked lump crab meat
2 thinly-sliced scallions
2 tablespoons homemade mayo
2 small Japanese cucumbers cut into matchsticks
1 pitted and sliced avocado
Juice from ½ lime
Handful of radish sprouts
½ teaspoon red pepper flakes
Sea salt
Black pepper

Directions:
1. Mix the mayo, crab, red pepper flakes, lime juice, and scallions with some salt and pepper.
2. Lay out a piece of nori (shiny-side down) and spoon 2 tablespoons of the crab filling on the left side of the seaweed and angled from the top left corner to bottom center.
3. Add a slice of avocado, sprouts, and cucumber to the filling before folding.
4. Fold the bottom left corner covering the filling, and then wrap the long part of the seaweed around the crab, like a cone.
5. Serve and enjoy!

Nutritional info (4 cones per serving)
Calories: 224
Protein: 30
Carbs: 7
Fat: 14
Fiber: 4

Beef and Rice-Stuffed Zucchini
Serves: 8
Time: About 45 minutes

This recipe features one of my favorite uses of cauliflower rice. It cooks with lean ground beef, absorbing all of the delicious juices before it all gets stuffed into a zucchini boat. It's super simple, but there's a lot of flavors going on, and it's very low-carb and paleo-approved.

Ingredients:
1 pound lean, grass-fed ground beef
4 big zucchinis
2 ½ cups cauliflower rice
3 tablespoons Dijon mustard
Sea salt to taste
Garlic powder to taste
Black pepper to taste

Directions:
1. Preheat your oven to 350-degrees and prepare the zucchini.
2. Trim off the ends and cut in half lengthwise.
3. Take out the seeds and inside of the zucchini, dice, and set aside.
4. To make the cauliflower rice, remove the florets from the cauliflower head and pulse in a processor until it resembles grains of rice.
5. In a skillet, cook the beef until it's nearly cooked through.
6. Add the cauliflower rice and zucchini insides that you diced up.
7. Cook for 2-3 minutes before adding the Dijon and spices.
8. Cook for another few minutes until everything is heated through.
9. Sprinkle salt and pepper on the cut zucchini and fill with the beef and rice.
10. Cover with foil and bake for 20 minutes.

11. Take off the foil and bake for 10 more minutes until the squash is tender.
12. Serve right away.

Nutritional info (1 zucchini boat w/ beef + rice per serving)
Calories: 146
Protein: 19
Carbs: 6
Fat: 4
Fiber: 1

Rosemary-Lemon Chicken + Potatoes

Serves: 8
Time: 1 hour, 5 minutes

There's very little work involved in this rustic chicken and potatoes dinner. You pretty much just throw everything into one dish and bake. Earthy rosemary goes so well with the bright acidity of lemon, and when you use a variety of chicken cuts (thighs, breasts, wings, etc.), there's something for everyone.

Ingredients:
10 pieces of mixed, skin-on chicken parts
1 pound baby red potatoes
2 minced garlic cloves
⅓ cup olive oil
½ onion, cut into chunks
2 lemons, one sliced and one juiced
1 tablespoon fresh rosemary
1 ½ teaspoons sea salt
½ teaspoon crushed red pepper flakes
½ teaspoon black pepper

Directions:
1. Preheat the oven to 400-degrees.
2. Grease a 13x9 baking dish.
3. Place the chicken pieces in the dish with the skin-side facing up, and add the potatoes, onions, and lemon slices.
4. In a bowl, mix the olive oil, garlic, lemon juice, rosemary, red pepper flakes, pepper, and salt.
5. Pour evenly over the chicken and potatoes.
6. Season again with salt and pepper before baking for 60 minutes.

Nutritional info (⅛ of the chicken pieces and potatoes)
Calories: 301
Protein: 34
Carbs: 11
Fat: 13
Fiber: 0

Steak Fajitas
Serves: 4
Time: 40

Fajitas are versatile, delicious, and great for summer. This recipe calls for steak, but you can substitute it for chicken if you would like, and keep the spices the same. I like to serve mine on some crisp lettuce, but chard or cabbage leaves work just as well.

Ingredients:
1 pound boneless beef steak cut into 1 ½-inch strips
1 large, sliced yellow onion
4 medium sliced garlic cloves
3 medium seeded and sliced bell peppers
2 large seeded and sliced jalapeno
4 tablespoons olive oil
1 seeded and sliced avocado
¼ cup fresh cilantro
2 teaspoons cumin
2 teaspoons chili powder
2 teaspoons garlic powder
2 teaspoons onion powder
½ teaspoon cayenne pepper
½ teaspoon sea salt
½ teaspoon black pepper

Directions:
1. In a bowl, mix the powdered spices with ½ cup water.
2. In a skillet, heat up two tablespoons of olive oil on medium-high.
3. Once hot, toss in the garlic and onions to sauté for 3-5 minutes.
4. When they are translucent, add two more tablespoons of oil, and the steak and jalapeno.
5. Once the meat is brown (5-7 minutes), add the spice mixture.

6. Reduce the heat to low-medium and simmer for 10 minutes, without a lid.
7. Turn up the heat back to medium and add the bell peppers. Cook for 3-5 minutes until they just become soft.
8. There shouldn't be much liquid left in the skillet.
9. Serve on a large leafy green with cilantro, a squirt of lime, avocado, and other toppings.

Nutritional info (¼ of the skillet in a leafy green)
Calories: 374
Protein: 26
Carbs: 10
Fat: 25
Fiber: 4

Macadamia Nut-Crusted Baked Chicken
Serves: 4
Time: 30 minutes

Just three ingredients. That's all you need to make this tender chicken with an amazing crust of macadamia nuts. I love using nuts as "breading," because they add great texture and great nutrition. Using mayo as a binder keeps the chicken super moist, and brings more flavor than an egg wash would.

Ingredients:
4 chicken breasts
4.3-ounces of chopped, raw Macadamia nuts
2 tablespoons homemade mayo

Directions:
1. Preheat your oven to 400-degrees and pat the chicken breasts dry.
2. Lay them on a baking sheet and brush with mayo.
3. Sprinkle the chopped nuts on top.
4. Bake for around 30 minutes, or until the chicken reaches 165-degrees and the nuts are brown.
5. Serve hot with dipping sauces, like more mayo, homemade ranch dressing, or homemade honey mustard!

Nutritional info (1 chicken breast per serving)
Calories: 486
Protein: 53

Carbs: 4
Fat: 30
Fiber: 2.4

Shrimp & Sausage Jambalaya

Serves: 8-10
Time: 45 minutes

Jambalaya brings to mind long, hot hours slaving over a stove and rich, deep flavors. With this recipe, you get all the flavors, but without the agonizing cooking time. The stew has all the essentials - shrimp, sausage, peppers, and seasonings like thyme, garlic, and bay leaves.

Ingredients:
1 pound shrimp
3 cups cauliflower rice
2 cups chicken stock
12-ounces Andouille sausage, cut into ¼ rounds
1 diced onion
1 cored and diced green bell pepper
1 cored and diced red bell pepper
14-ounces diced tomatoes w/ liquid
1 cup diced celery
2 pressed garlic cloves
2 bay leaves
¼ cup chopped green onions
¼ cup fresh parsley
2 tablespoons tomato paste
½ juiced lemon
1 tablespoon olive oil
1 tablespoon grass-fed butter
1 teaspoon dried oregano
1 teaspoon sea salt
1 teaspoon dried thyme
1 teaspoon black pepper
¼ teaspoon cayenne

Directions:
1. In a big pot, heat olive oil.
2. Add the sausages and brown.
3. Take out the sausage and set aside for later.

4. To the same pot, add butter, onion, peppers, and celery, and sauté until the onion becomes clear.
5. Add the diced tomatoes, cayenne, garlic, oregano, thyme, and tomato paste and cook until the herbs blend in with the other ingredients.
6. Pour in the chicken stock and bring the pot to a boil.
7. Return the sausage rounds to the pot, along with the bay leaves, salt, and pepper.
8. Return to a boil before reducing the heat and simmering for 15 minutes.
9. Add 2 tablespoons of green onions, 2 tablespoons of parsley, shrimp, and lemon juice.
10. Stir and then cover the pot before removing it from the heat, so everything cooks by steaming.
11. After 15 minutes, pick out the bay leaves.
12. Serve over cauliflower rice and garnished with the rest of the parsley and green onion.

Nutritional info (⅛ of the stew per serving)
Calories: 426
Protein: 25
Carbs: 52
Fat: 12
Fiber: 5

One-Pot Mediterranean Chicken
Serves: 4
Time: About 20 minutes

I love one-pot recipes. It keeps everything simple and tidy, and I don't have to watch a bunch of pots or skillets each cooking at different temperatures and times. This recipe is for Mediterranean chicken with artichoke hearts, tomatoes, mushrooms, fresh spinach, and Kalamata olives. It is truly like taking a bite out of Greece or Italy. For speed reasons, I use pre-cooked chicken breasts, which you can make the morning or even night before, and reduce your cooking time for the evening's meal.

Ingredients:
1 pound pre-cooked chicken breasts
8 ounces of artichoke hearts
8 ounces sliced mushrooms
3 diced Roma tomatoes

2-3 minced garlic cloves
½ diced yellow onion
½ cup chopped sun-dried tomatoes
⅓ cup chopped Kalamata olives
Few handfuls of fresh spinach
2-3 tablespoons olive oil
2 tablespoons fresh basil
1 tablespoon balsamic vinegar
1 teaspoon dried parsley
1 teaspoon dried oregano
Sea salt and pepper

Directions:
1. Heat 1 tablespoon of olive oil in a large skillet and sauté the onions for 3-4 minutes.
2. Add the minced garlic and sauté for another minute.
3. Next, add the mushrooms and cook until the mushrooms become golden. Season with salt and pepper.
4. Pour in another tablespoon of olive oil and a tablespoon of balsamic vinegar.
5. Add the Roma tomatoes, sun-dried tomatoes, olives, and artichoke hearts.
6. Toss in the oregano and parsley, and stir.
7. Put the chicken and spinach in the pan and cook until the chicken heats up.
8. Taste, and season with more salt and pepper if necessary.
9. Serve with a garnish of fresh, chopped basil.

Nutritional info (1 chicken breast w/ ¼ of the skillet per serving)
Calories: 296
Protein: 30
Carbs: 15
Fat: 13
Fiber: 4

Deconstructed Shepherd's Pie
Serves: 4
Time: 45 minutes

Shepherd's Pie is a great comfort food dish - a savory pie topped with mashed red potatoes and filled with meat, mushrooms, carrots, and green beans. For this recipe, however, you separate out the pie components, so you don't have to use dough to hold it all together. All the flavors are still there - it's just easier to make.

Ingredients:
1 ½ pounds beef steak
4 tablespoons apple cider vinegar
2 tablespoons olive oil
2 teaspoons thyme
2 teaspoons dried rosemary
Black pepper to taste
1 pound fresh green beans
6 large carrots cut into 1-inch pieces
2 cups baby Portobello mushrooms
1 cup water
¾ cup chicken broth
6-ounces tomato paste
1 teaspoon garlic powder
1 teaspoon thyme
1 teaspoon rosemary
1 teaspoon onion powder
18 small, halved red potatoes
8 cups water
2 ¼ cups chicken broth, divided
2 tablespoons ghee
1 teaspoon garlic powder
Sea salt and black pepper to taste

Directions:
1. Cook the vegetables and mashed potatoes first.
2. Focus on the second ingredient list. In a saucepan, mix the water, chicken broth, and tomato paste. Bring to a boil.
3. Add the garlic powder, thyme, rosemary, and onion powder and stir.
4. Throw in the mushrooms, carrots, and green beans.
5. Cover the saucepan and let it boil for 10 minutes.
6. Reduce the heat and cook for another 15-20 minutes, until the carrots are soft.
7. While the saucepan is covered and boiling for 10 minutes (before you reduce the heat), begin the mashed potatoes.
8. In a big pot, bring 1 ½ cups of chicken broth and water to a boil. The list of ingredients begins with "18 small, halved red potatoes."

9. Add the potatoes and cook for about 20 minutes or until they're soft.
10. Drain the pot liquid and move the potatoes to a bowl.
11. Add the rest of the broth, along with the ghee.
12. Mash the potatoes, with the skin on.
13. Season with garlic powder, salt, and pepper.
14. Now, the steaks. Let the meat rest at room temperature.
15. In a bowl, coat the steaks in a mixture of rosemary, thyme, pepper, and apple cider vinegar from the first ingredient list.
16. Heat a skillet.
17. When hot, add the ghee and steaks.
18. Cook for 3 minutes on each side on medium high.
19. Reduce the heat and cook on medium-low for 5-7 minutes.
20. Distribute the potatoes, veggies, and steaks evenly on four plates, and enjoy!

Nutritional info (1 plate per serving)
Calories: 384
Protein: 28
Carbs: 30
Fat: 16
Fiber: 3

Baked Red Snapper
Serves: 2
Time: 45 minutes

Red snapper is a good source of lean protein, vitamin A, and the antioxidant selenium, which strengthens white blood cells. Because red snapper is a fish that tends to absorb mercury, you shouldn't eat it all the time, but it's perfectly fine to eat it 2-3 times a month for something different than salmon, tuna, and so on.

Ingredients:
1 pound red snapper fish fillets
4 onions, cut into ½-inch chunks
1 cup cilantro
1 chopped tomato
1 juiced lime
½ chopped red bell pepper
½ juiced lemon
1 small chopped Anaheim pepper
1 teaspoon chili powder

Directions:
1.   Preheat the oven to 350-degrees
2.   Put the fish fillets in a baking dish.
3.   Mix the lemon juice, lime juice, and chili powder in a bowl and pour over the fish.
4.   Marinate for 10 minutes, turning the fish a couple of times so it marinates evenly.
5.   Combine the chopped onions, peppers, and tomato, and toss over the fish.
6.   Cover the baking dish and bake for 20-30 minutes until the fish has a flaky center.
7.   Rest the fish for 4 minutes.
8.   Serve with a garnish of fresh cilantro.

Nutritional info (½ pound of snapper w/ topping per serving)
Calories: 362
Protein: 52
Carbs: 31
Fat: 3
Fiber: 0

Bison Chili
Serves: 4
Time: 2 hours

There are countless variations on chili, and it can be hard to pick a favorite. Here's another one to add to the list - bison chili. It is high in protein and iron, but has less fat and overall calories than beef, and less cholesterol than chicken. You simmer this hearty meal for an hour, so all the flavors can really deepen.

Ingredients:
1 ¾ pounds of ground bison
3 diced celery stalks
2 sliced garlic cloves
½ diced yellow onion
12-ounces of salsa
8-ounces diced tomatoes
7-ounces mild green chiles
1 tablespoon coconut oil
2 teaspoons sea salt
2 teaspoons cumin

2 teaspoons chili powder
2 teaspoons thyme

Directions:
1. Choose a heavy-bottomed soup pot and heat it over medium-high.
2. Add the coconut oil to warm up.
3. Put in the garlic, celery, and onions to sauté for 3-4 minutes.
4. Once the onions are clear, add the meat, thyme, chili powder, and cumin.
5. For 5-6 minutes, stir the chili.
6. Add the salt, green chiles, tomatoes, and salsa.
7. Simmer for at least an hour.
8. Serve hot!

Nutritional info (1 cup per serving)
Calories: 215
Protein: 16
Carbs: 29
Fat: 5
Fiber: 10

Spicy Roasted Vegetable Soup
Serves: 4
Time: 55 minutes

Root vegetables are extremely healthy and plentiful during the winter. This soup uses some of the more underrated roots and cooks turnips, parsnips, and rutabaga with bacon and spices like cumin and red pepper flakes. To make this soup vegetarian, just eliminate the bacon.

Ingredients:
4 cups organic or homemade chicken broth
4 tablespoons olive oil
4 diced slices of bacon
2 medium-sized peeled and diced turnips
2 minced garlic cloves
2 tablespoons arrowroot powder
1 chopped green onion
1 peeled and diced parsnip
1 peeled and diced rutabaga
1 diced yellow onion

½ teaspoon crushed red pepper flakes
½ teaspoon cumin
Sea salt and black pepper to taste

Directions:
1. Preheat your oven to 400-degrees.
2. Mix the vegetables with cumin and olive oil.
3. Bake the veggies on a baking sheet for 25-30 minutes.
4. Cook the bacon in a large pot over medium-heat.
5. When crisp, remove and add the onions.
6. Once the onion is soft, add the roasted vegetables, garlic, and red pepper flakes.
7. In a separate bowl, mix the broth with arrowroot powder.
8. Pour into the pot and bring to a boil.
9. When the pot begins to boil, turn off the heat.
10. Puree the soup until smooth.
11. Stir in the bacon.
12. Serve hot with chopped green onions as a garnish.

Nutritional info (¼ soup recipe per serving)
Calories: 256
Protein: 6
Carbs: 18
Fat: 18
Fiber: 7

Lamb Chops w/ Pistachios and Wilted Arugula
Serves: 4
Time: 20 minutes

Who says gourmet dinners need to take hours and hours? This lamb chop recipe doesn't even take a half-hour and only uses one skillet. It's a great option for holiday dinners at home when you want to focus on your family, and not cooking.

Ingredients:
4 lamb chops
4 cups baby arugula
2 diced celery stalks
2 tablespoons olive oil
½ cup shelled pistachios
Sea salt and black pepper to taste

Directions:
1. Heat the olive oil in a heavy-bottomed skillet, big enough to fit all four lamb chops.
2. Add the celery and sauté until they are soft.
3. Season the lamb chops with pepper and salt before adding them to the skillet.
4. Cook until they are brown and an internal temp of 145-degrees.
5. Plate the lamb chops and add the arugula to the pan.
6. Cook until they wilt and quickly plate on top of the lamb chops.
7. Serve with the pistachios sprinkled on top.

Nutritional info (1 lamb chop w/ arugula and nuts per serving)
Calories: 431
Protein: 40
Carbs: 6
Fat: 27
Fiber: 4

Baked Salmon w/ Pecans + Rosemary
Serves: 2
Time: 20 minutes

Here is another simple yet seemingly-gourmet dish that only takes 20 minutes. With only 5 ingredients, you can serve your significant other (or someone you *hope* will be your significant other) a beautiful, unique dish you can't find at every restaurant.

Ingredients:
¾ pound of skin-on salmon fillets
2 tablespoons coconut oil
2 tablespoons chopped pecans
1 tablespoon chopped, fresh rosemary
¼ teaspoon sea salt

Directions:
1. Preheat your oven to 350-degrees.
2. Grease a baking pan with the coconut oil and lay the salmon down skin down.
3. Sprinkle the fish with the rosemary, pecans, and salt.
4. Bake for 12-15 minutes, until the salmon is flaky.
5. Serve with a veggie side, like steamed green beans.

Nutritional info (½ salmon recipe per serving)
Calories: 370
Protein: 32
Carbs: 1
Fat: 27
Fiber: .8

Meatless Apple Burgers

Serves: 3
Time: About 20 minutes

If you like having a sweet dish every now and then for dinner, like chocolate chip pancakes, you'll love these apple burgers. They're made with plantain flour, which is gluten-free, and seasonings like nutmeg and cinnamon. I would suggest serving the burgers without a bun, on top of a fresh green salad.

Ingredients:
2 large organic eggs
1 cup minced apple
1 cup plantain flour
1-2 tablespoons grass-fed butter
½ lemon, juiced
1 ½ teaspoons cinnamon
¾ teaspoon baking soda
A pinch of nutmeg
A pinch of cloves

Directions:
1. In a bowl, mix the flour, nutmeg, cloves, baking soda, and cinnamon.
2. In a separate bowl, whisk the eggs.
3. Add the lemon juice, apple, and eggs to the dry mixture and stir.
4. In a cast-iron skillet, melt 1 tablespoon of butter.
5. While that heats up, form a tablespoon-sized patty from the apple mixture.
6. About three patties will fit in the skillet at one time. Cook for 3-5 minutes on each side until brown.
7. Plate the cooked patties and cook the other three.
8. Serve with a drizzle of pure maple syrup or homemade mustard.

Calories: 354
Protein: 17
Carbs: 48
Fat: 9
Fiber: 1

Ginger Beef + Noodle Stir Fry
Serves: 4
Time: 30 minutes

Beef and noodle stir-fry is one of the many dishes you can find at just about any Chinese eatery, but like most Chinese food we've talked about, it's got MSG in it, and the pasta is probably not up to the whole-food code. In this homemade version, we eliminate anything artificial, and replace noodles with zucchini.

Ingredients:
1 ½ pounds sliced flank steak
2 medium-sized zucchini
4 tablespoons coconut aminos
3 tablespoons sesame oil
2 medium-sized green onions, sliced
2 minced garlic cloves
2 tablespoons fresh chopped cilantro
1 juiced lime
1 tablespoon sea salt
1 teaspoon red pepper flakes
1 teaspoon fresh, grated ginger

Directions:
1. In a large bowl, whisk the lime juice, garlic, ginger, and coconut aminos.
2. Add the meat and marinate for 10 minutes.
3. With a spiral slicer (or julienne peeler), cut the zucchini into noodles.
4. Lay the strips on a paper towel and sprinkle with salt. Rest for 10 minutes.
5. In a skillet, heat the sesame oil and add the pepper flakes and green onions to sauté for 1 minute.
6. Add the beef and cook until browned.

ontinue to stir until the beef is cooked
d the zucchini is tender.
d serve with the cilantro!

erving)

Fibe.

Slow-Cooker Stuffed Cabbage Rolls

Serves: 5
Time: 7+ hours

Cabbage is one of the world's healthiest foods, but it can be tricky to find interesting ways of serving it. How about wrapped around seasoned beef and cooked for 7 hours? The result is tender, juicy, and very low-carb.

Ingredients:
1 head of green cabbage
1 pound grass-fed ground beef
1 pound organic carrots
3 cups salsa
2 tablespoons dried oregano
½ teaspoon sea salt

Directions:
1. Start to boil water in a saucepan big enough to fit the cabbage leaves.
2. Prepare the cabbage by piercing the head of the cabbage with a sharp knife, and moving the knife in a circular fashion.
3. Carefully pull off the leaves.
4. When the water is boiling, put 3 leaves in the water and boil until they become a brighter green color.
5. Take out the leaves and plate.
6. Finish the leaves.
7. Prepare the carrots by chopping off the ends, peeling, and shredding.
8. Break up the ground beef and add to the bowl of shredded carrots.
9. Season with oregano and salt, and mix with your hands.

10. Spread out the cabbage leaves and spoon ¼ of the meat mixture on the leaf's stem end.
11. Sprinkle with salt.
12. Fold both sides of the leaf over the meat and roll from the stem to the other end.
13. Put the cabbage rolls (seam-side down) into a crockpot.
14. Pour salsa on top of the rolls and cook on low for 6-7 hours.
15. The meat insides should reach a temp of 160-degrees.
16. Serve and enjoy!

Nutritional info (4 rolls per serving)
Calories: 349
Protein: 23
Carbs: 33
Fat: 10
Fiber: 2

Three-Pepper Stew w/ Pork
Serves: 4
Time: 3 hours

Ah, there's nothing quite like a stew that's been simmering for a few hours. I'm a big fan of stews with shorter cooking time, but sometimes, it's actually more practical to be able to start dinner a little earlier in the day, and then have it cook itself for a few hours before serving. This stew uses red, green, and jalapeno peppers, and tender pork shoulder chunks seasoned with cumin, chili powder, and basil.

Ingredients:
2 pounds pork shoulder, cut into chunks
4 cups chicken broth
3 minced garlic cloves
2 medium-sized seeded and diced jalapenos
1 seeded and diced red bell pepper
1 seeded and diced green bell pepper
1 diced onion
½ cup chopped fresh basil
3 tablespoons organic tomato paste
2 tablespoons olive oil
1 juiced lime
1 teaspoon chili powder
½ teaspoon whole cumin seeds

Sea salt to taste
Black pepper to taste

Directions:
1. Heat the olive oil and brown the pork on both sides.
2. When brown, remove from the pan.
3. Toss in the onions and peppers and sauté until softened.
4. Mix in the cumin, chili powder, and garlic.
5. After 1 minute, put the pork back in the pan.
6. Pour in the broth and tomato paste.
7. When the pan is boiling, reduce to a simmer.
8. Simmer for 2 hours until the pork has become tender.
9. With a fork, shred the pork and stir in the lime juice.
10. Season with salt and pepper, and serve!

Nutritional info (1/4 stew per serving)
Calories: 734
Protein: 57
Carbs: 10
Fat: 48
Fiber: 1

Rabbit Cacciatore w/ Meatballs + Mashed Sweet Potatoes
Serves: 2-3
Time: About an hour

Though a lot of people feel weird about eating rabbit, which is a shame, because it is a good source of lean protein, it's low in fat, and low in calories, especially when compared to beef. If you're comfortable eating rabbit, this is a great recipe for it, which also includes pork meatballs and delicious mashed sweet potatoes.

Ingredients:
1 fresh rabbit
1 pound ground pork
3 cups chopped tomatoes
2-3 large, peeled and chopped sweet potatoes
1 chopped onion
1 minced garlic clove
1 cup water
⅓ cup dry white wine
3.5 ounces of sliced shiitake mushrooms
3 tablespoons fresh thyme

3 tablespoons fresh rosemary
2 tablespoons extra virgin olive oil
Garlic powder to taste
Black pepper to taste
Sea salt to taste
Onion powder to taste

Directions:

1. Cut the rabbit into pieces.
2. In a large pot, cover the sweet potatoes with water and bring to a boil.
3. Once boiling, reduce the heat and simmer until you can pierce the potatoes with a fork.
4. In the meantime, in another big pot, heat the oil on medium-high.
5. Take the rabbit pieces and season on both sides with pepper and salt.
6. Brown the pieces in the boat and move to a plate.
7. In this same pot, add onions and garlic and sauté for 1-2 minutes on medium.
8. Add the water, wine, and tomatoes.
9. Deglaze the pot before bringing the pot to a boil.
10. The sweet potatoes should be done by now, so drain them and keep them covered on a plate.
11. Put the rabbit back in the pot with the tomatoes, onions, and garlic, and stir.
12. Reduce the heat to medium and simmer for a half hour.
13. To prepare the meatballs, roll the ground meat in your hands.
14. Heat some more olive oil in a skillet and add the meatballs.
15. Season generously with the dried spices and cover.
16. Cook for 5 minutes, stir, and then cover.
17. Take out the rabbit and plate.
18. Add the mushrooms and herbs to the pot and stir.
19. Simmer and reduce for 5 minutes.
20. Add the rabbit back to the pot, along with the meatballs, and simmer for 5 minutes until everything is blended.
21. Mash the sweet potatoes.
22. Serve by scooping a heaping spoon of sweet potatoes on a plate and topping with 3-5 meatballs and a piece of rabbit.

Nutritional info (¼ recipe per serving)
Calories: 785

Protein: 81
Carbs: 27
Fat: 36
Fiber: 2

Steamed Plaice Rolls
Serves: 2
Time: 30 minutes

Plaice, which is a tender white fish, is a zero-carb, high-protein food with low fat *and* sodium. It is best to buy this fish as fresh as possible. When it comes to the roll part, the fish sometimes falls apart as it cooks, but that's okay, it will still taste great.

Ingredients:
1 pound plaice fillets
1 ½ cups vegetable broth
2 carrots, cut into matchsticks
2 parsnips, cut into matchsticks
2 tablespoons coconut oil
2 sliced leeks, white and light green parts only
1 teaspoon thyme
¼ teaspoon sea salt
Black pepper to taste

Directions:
1. Cut the plaice fillets in half, lengthwise.
2. Season each side with fresh pepper and sea salt, and roll.
3. Heat a sauté pan over medium-high and add coconut oil.
4. Sauté the parsnips, leeks, and carrots for 5 minutes.
5. Place the rolls on top of the veggies in the pan, and cover.
6. The fish should steam for 8-10 minutes until the fish is tender.
7. Divide the fish and veggie mixture between two parts, and enjoy!

Nutritional info (½ pound fish + veggies per serving)
Calories: 553
Protein: 4
Carbs: 44
Fat: 14
Fiber: 7

Egg Drop Soup
Serves: 4
Time: 45 minutes

Egg drop soup traditionally comes from China, and consists of wisps of egg in hot chicken broth. Add-ins can include chicken, tofu, scallions, and bean sprouts. It is a great alternative to chicken noodle soup when you're sick, especially when you use healing homemade organic chicken broth and fresh ginger.

Ingredients:
8 cups homemade chicken broth
6 organic eggs
2 diced celery stalks
1 diced yellow onion
3 tablespoons arrowroot powder
3 tablespoons water
1 tablespoon coconut oil
1 teaspoon coconut aminos
1 teaspoon sea salt
¼ teaspoon fresh grated ginger
¼ teaspoon sesame oil

Directions:
1. Begin by melting the coconut oil in a big pot.
2. When hot, sauté the onions and celery for 15 minutes.
3. Pour in the broth.
4. Add in the sesame oil, coconut aminos, and ginger.
5. Let the soup come to a boil.
6. In a separate bowl, mix the water with the arrowroot powder.
7. Pour into the pot and cook for 10 minutes or until the soup has thickened.
8. In another bowl, whisk the eggs.
9. When the soup is thick, pour the eggs slowly into the pot. The eggs should become like streamers or ribbons.
10. Serve with a garnish of scallions and salt and pepper to taste.

Nutritional info (¼ soup pot per serving)
Calories: 73
Protein: 7.52
Carbs: 1
Fat: 3.8

Fiber: 0

Grilled Lobster w/ Cilantro-Chile Butter
Serves: 4
Time: About 18-20 minutes

Don't be intimidated by this recipe because it uses live lobsters. Going through the initial prep is well-worth it, because you know the lobster is as fresh as it can get. Grilling the lobster is done in a snap, and the cilantro-chile butter makes the idea of using just regular melted butter absurd.

Ingredients:
2 (2-pound) live lobsters
¼ cup olive oil
4-ounces unsalted, softened, grass-fed butter
4 seeded and minced Holland chiles
3 tablespoons minced cilantro
1 zested and quartered lime
Sea salt and black pepper to taste

Directions:
1. First, chill the lobsters for 20 minutes so they become numb.
2. Place the lobster on your cutting board, belly-side down, and place the tip of a very sharp knife behind the lobster's eyes, at the center of the "cross" shape the lobster's body has.
3. With a quick, confident motion, cut through the head moving forward.
4. The lobster is immediately killed; any movement is just reflex.
5. Turn the lobsters over and cut in half lengthwise.
6. Clean out the innards (which are yellow-green) and cut off the claws.
7. Move the lobster halves to a baking sheet, with the shell-side facing down.
8. Crack open the lobster claws and put them on the sheet, as well.
9. Drizzle olive oil, salt, and pepper unto the lobster parts.
10. Heat your grill to medium-high.
11. Put the lobster halves (with the flesh-side down) and claws on the grill and cook for 5 minutes.
12. In a small bowl, mix the butter, chiles, cilantro, and lime zest together.

13. Turn the lobsters over, exposing the cooked flesh, and brush with the cilantro-chile butter.
14. Keep cooking on that side for 3 minutes.
15. Serve with the quartered lime wedges.

Nutritional info (1 lobster half/1 pound lobster per serving)
Calories: 619
Protein: 60
Carbs: 5
Fat: 38
Fiber: 0

Honey + Poppy-Seed Cornish Hens
Serves: 4
Time: 1 hour, 45 minutes

Cornish hens come at a higher price than other poultry, but you can feed four people with just two. They present beautifully, and are a great option for Thanksgiving or other holiday meals when you want to try something a little different. This recipe blends the bird with the sweetness of honey, the nuttiness of poppy seeds, and fresh spiciness of ginger.

Ingredients:
2 Rock cornish hens
⅓ cup raw honey
1 tablespoon poppy seeds
1 ½ teaspoons mustard powder
¾ teaspoon ground ginger
½ teaspoon sea salt
½ teaspoon ground black pepper

Directions:
1. Preheat your oven to 350-degrees and grease a shallow roasting pan with some olive oil.
2. Prepare the birds by cutting them in half and putting them skin-side down in the pan.
3. Season with salt and pepper.
4. In a small bowl, mix the mustard, ginger, honey, and poppy seeds.
5. Slather both sides of the hens with the mixture.
6. Roast uncovered for 1 hour, turning once about halfway through the cooking time.

Calories: 441
Protein: 29.7
Carbs: 24.7
Fat: 24.9
Fiber: .6

Maple-Glazed Turkey Roast
Serves: 6
Time: 1 hour, 50 minutes

We associate turkey with Thanksgiving, and very often, there's just one recipe you follow. For something a little more unique, I love this maple-infused turkey roast that is rich with seasonings like onion powder, thyme, paprika, and cayenne. It's so good, you'll be making it when it's *not* Thanksgiving.

Ingredients:
1 (3-pound) thawed boneless turkey breast roast
½ cup pure maple syrup
1 teaspoon ground paprika
½ teaspoon pepper
½ teaspoon sea salt
½ teaspoon garlic powder
½ teaspoon onion powder
1 pinch cayenne pepper

Directions:
1. Preheat your oven to 325-degrees.
2. Take off the plastic netting and wrap from the turkey roast, leaving on the string part.
3. Rinse and pat the turkey dry.
4. In a bowl, mix the seasonings and maple syrup.
5. Brush over the turkey roast.
6. Put the roast, skin-side up, and set on a baking rack that's in a roasting pan.
7. Roast with occasional basting for about 1 ½ hours.
8. Wrap in foil, and rest for 10 minutes before cutting off the string netting.
9. Slice and enjoy!

Nutritional info (⅙ roast per serving)

Calories: 351
Protein: 40
Carbs: 32.9
Fat: 5.9
Fiber: 0

Chapter 11 - Condiments + Dressings

Classic Ketchup
Makes: 1 cup
Time: 25 minutes

If you're committed to a whole-food diet, you need a solid ketchup recipe. Ketchup from big brands is packed with artificial colors and flavors, while organic ones can be costly. It's much easier to just make your own.

Ingredients:
1 garlic clove
½ small onion
½ cup (+ 2 tablespoons) of organic tomato paste
⅓ cup water
¼ cup raw organic honey
⅓ cup apple cider vinegar
¾ teaspoon fine-grain sea salt

Directions:
1. Puree the garlic and onion in a food processor until *completely* smooth.
2. In a saucepan, combine the garlic/onion puree with the honey, tomato paste, apple cider vinegar, salt, and water.
3. Whisk together until smooth and heat until it begins to boil.
4. Reduce the heat and simmer for 20 minutes.
5. The ketchup should thicken.
6. After 20 minutes, remove from the heat, cover, and let it cool to room temperature.
7. Store in the fridge in an airtight container.

Nutritional info (1 tablespoon per serving)
Calories: 26
Protein: .5
Carbs: 6.7
Fat: 0
Fiber: 0

Simple Yellow Mustard

Makes: ½ cup
Time: 15 minutes

After ketchup, mustard is probably one of the most common condiments you'd miss on a whole-food diet. There are lots of types of mustards - honey, spicy, and so on - but we'll just stick with classic yellow.

Ingredients:
½ cup water
½ cup mustard powder
Sea salt to taste

Directions:
1. Whisk the water and mustard powder together.
2. Let the mustard rest for 15 minutes while it thickens.

Cooking Tip:

For a deeper flavor profile, you can add ingredients like fresh parsley, lemon zest, or vinegar.

Nutritional info (1 tablespoon per serving)
Calories: 39
Protein: 0
Carbs: 1
Fat: 0
Fiber: 0

Worcestershire Sauce
Makes: Just over ½ cup
Time: 10 minutes

This recipe is kind of cheating, because it doesn't use the fermented anchovies traditionally used in the sauce, but this is much easier, and it tastes just the same.

Ingredients:
½ cup apple cider vinegar
2 tablespoons coconut aminos
2 tablespoons water
¼ teaspoon mustard powder

¼ teaspoon ground ginger
¼ teaspoon onion powder
¼ teaspoon garlic powder
⅛ teaspoon black pepper
⅛ teaspoon cinnamon

Directions:
1. Mix all the ingredients in a saucepan over medium-low heat.
2. Stir while the mixture comes to a boil.
3. When it starts to boil, reduce the heat and simmer for 1 minute.
4. Remove from the heat and let the sauce cool.
5. Store in an airtight container in the fridge.

Nutritional info (1 tablespoon per serving)
Calories: 5
Protein: 0
Carbs: 1
Fat: 0
Fiber: 0

Classic Horseradish
Makes: 1 cup
Time: 3-7 days/5 minute actual cook time

Horseradish is pungent and strong-tasting. It packs a big punch in a small package. Traditional horseradish is fermented, so you need to get a packet of vegetable culture starter to ferment the horseradish. There are recipes that skip this process, but for a true horseradish taste, I recommend this recipe.

Ingredients:
2-4 tablespoons of water
1 cup peeled and finely-chopped horseradish root
1 packet vegetable culture starter
1 ½ teaspoons sea salt

Directions:
1. Pulse the culture, salt, and horseradish root in a food processor.
2. Add 3 tablespoons of water and blend again for 3 minutes until a paste forms.

3. Store the paste in a glass jar and add enough water to fill the jar.
4. Cover loosely with the lid and store in a warm place for 3-7 days.
5. Once the fermentation has finished, store in the fridge.

Nutritional info (1 tablespoon per serving)
Calories: 7
Protein: 0
Carbs: 1
Fat: 0
Fiber: 0

Homemade Mayo
Makes: About 1 cup
Time: 1 hour

You need mayonnaise for a lot of the recipes included in this book, so here is the recipe you should use. It's very simple, so you can keep making it for all your condiment and recipe needs.

Ingredients:
1 cup light olive oil
1 room-temperature egg
2 tablespoons fresh lemon juice
½ teaspoon dry mustard
½ teaspoon sea salt

Directions:
1. Blend the egg and lemon juice together.
2. Wait for about an hour, until the mixture reaches room temperature.
3. Add the mustard and salt.
4. Blend again, and slowly pour in the olive oil.
5. When it has the texture you want, it is ready to use.
6. Store in the fridge for up to a week.

Nutritional info (1 tablespoon per serving)
Calories: 111
Protein: .5
Carbs: 0
Fat: 12.5
Fiber: 0

Ranch Dressing
Makes: About ½ cup

Ranch is a delicious condiment that can be used on chicken and veggies alike. It can easily be mixed with other ingredients like Sriracha for a new taste, so by having a basic recipe memorized, you really have a handful of condiments in your book.

Ingredients:
½ cup homemade mayo
½ cup coconut milk
1 teaspoon dill
1 teaspoon garlic powder
½ teaspoon onion powder
Salt and pepper to taste

Directions:
1. Whisk all the ingredients together.
2. Season to taste with salt and pepper.
3. Keep in the fridge for up to a week.

Nutritional info (1 tablespoon per serving)
Calories: 65
Protein: 0
Carbs: 0
Fat: 0
Fiber: 0

Creamy Caesar Dressing
Makes: 1 cup
Time: Less than 5 minutes

Homemade Caesar dressing just can't be compared to the store-bought kind. The flavors are real, complex, and with only two steps, it's so easy to make.

Ingredients:
4 whole anchovy filets
2 cloves garlic
½ cup extra virgin olive oil
1 tablespoon Dijon mustard
1 egg yolk

1 juiced lemon
1 teaspoon black pepper

<u>Directions:</u>
1. Mix all the ingredients (excluding the olive oil) in a food processor.
2. Once blended, slowly add the oil.
3. Store in the fridge.

<u>Nutritional info (1 tablespoon per serving)</u>
Calories: 63
Protein: 0
Carbs: .5
Fat: 7
Fiber: 0

Simple French Dressing
Makes: ¾ cup
Time: Less than 1 minute

Many French dressing recipes use Ketchup and lots of sugar to get the flavor we're used to from the bottle, but this all-natural version sticks to the basics: tomato paste, dry mustard, onion, and red wine vinegar.

<u>Ingredients:</u>
7 tablespoons olive oil
⅓ cup red wine vinegar
2 teaspoons water
1 teaspoon unsalted tomato paste
½ teaspoon chopped onion
½ teaspoon dry mustard
¼ teaspoon ground white pepper

<u>Directions:</u>
1. In a jar, mix all the ingredients and shake well.
2. Serve right away or chill in the fridge.

<u>Nutritional info (1 tablespoon per serving)</u>
Calories: 47
Protein: .4
Carbs: 25
Fat: 5.2

Fiber: 0

Classic Lemon Vinaigrette
Makes: About ¾ cup
Time: Less than a minute

A vinaigrette dressing is defined by its use of oil and vinegar, though as you will see, any acid can work in place of vinegar. When it comes to vinaigrettes, lemon is one of the most popular. It's extremely easy to make it, and only takes five ingredients.

Ingredients:
¾ cup extra-virgin olive oil
3 tablespoons fresh lemon juice
½ teaspoon Dijon mustard
Sea salt to taste
Black pepper to taste

Directions:
1. Combine all the ingredients except the oil in a blender.
2. Add the oil slowly, while running the blender.
3. Store in the fridge.

Cooking Tip:
Vinaigrettes tend to separate, with the oil floats on top. Always shake a container of vinaigrette before using.

Nutritional info (1 tablespoon per serving)
Calories: 40
Protein: 0
Carbs: 1
Fat: 4
Fiber: 0

Orange-Sesame Dressing
Makes: About ¾ cup
Time: Less than 1 minute

If sweeter dressings are your thing, this Asian-inspired orange and sesame recipe is one you'll have to try out. It uses the juice from 2 big, fresh oranges, sesame seeds, and Asian mustard, which you can probably find at most groceries in the ethnic food section.

Ingredients:
½ cup orange juice (2 big oranges)
⅓ cup white vinegar
1 minced garlic clove
3 tablespoons sesame oil
2 tablespoons sesame seeds
1 tablespoon Asian mustard
¼ teaspoon sea salt

Directions:
1. Whisk the orange juice, sesame seeds, vinegar, mustard, sugar, salt, and garlic together.
2. Slowly add the sesame oil by whisking.
3. Store in the fridge.

Nutritional info (1 tablespoon per serving)
Calories: 57
Protein: 1
Carbs: 4
Fat: 5
Fiber: 0

Chapter 12 - Sweet + Salty Snacks

Simple Turkey-Apple Meatballs
Serves: 8
Time: 35 minutes

These meatballs are sweetened with applesauce and cinnamon, and provide a powerful pop of protein and fiber between lunch and dinner on your longest work days.

Ingredients:
1 ¼ pounds ground turkey
1 cup of organic applesauce
½ cup ground flaxseed
½ cup almond flour
½ tablespoon sea salt
½ teaspoon cinnamon

Directions:
1. Preheat the oven to 350-degrees.
2. Put the ground meat in a bowl, along with the apples, almond flour, salt, flaxseed, and cinnamon.
3. Mix with your hands.
4. Mold the meat into 1.5-inch meatballs and place in a greased muffin tin.
5. Bake for 30 minutes.

Nutritional info (⅛ recipe per serving)
Calories: 244
Protein: 22
Carbs: 10
Fat: 14
Fiber: 4

Kiwi Chips
Serves: 4
Time: 12 hours, 15 minutes

Kiwis are rich in antioxidants and other nutrients, while remaining low-calorie. Snacking on these kiwi chips is a great alternative to regular dried fruit or fruit snacks.

Ingredients:
4 kiwis

Directions:
1. Peel the kiwis with a vegetable peeler.
2. Slice into ¼-inch slices.
3. If you have dehydrator, dehydrate at 135-degrees for 6-12 hours until slightly chewy.
4. For the oven, bake on a cookie sheet on the lowest possible temperature. Check after 4 hours.

Nutritional info (1 kiwi per serving)
Calories: 48
Protein: 1
Carbs: 11
Fat: 0
Fiber: 2.1

Buffalo Cashews
Serves: 4
Time: 2 hours, 30 minutes

Rich, crunchy cashews are married with buffalo-style seasonings for a great take on bar nuts. They take a little while to prepare because of the cashew soaking, but hands-on time is limited.

Ingredients:
2 cups raw cashews
¾ cup Sriracha
⅓ cup olive oil
½ teaspoon garlic powder
⅛ teaspoon turmeric powder

Directions:
1. Mix the hot sauce and olive in a cup, and pour over the cashews.
2. Soak for at least 2 hours. If you want them really hot, go up to 4 hours, but no longer.
3. When the soaking is over, preheat the oven to 325-degrees.

4. Arrange the cashews on a baking sheet and bake for 30-35 minutes. Stir every 10 minutes.

Cooking Tip:

For crunchier cashews, drain the cashews through a colander before putting in the oven to drain the extra sauce. Also, flip every 6-8 minutes instead of every 10, and take out after 20-25 minutes of baking.

Nutritional info (½ cup per serving)
Calories: 384
Protein: 7
Carbs: 18
Fat: 32
Fiber: 2

Jalapeno Pumpkin Seeds
Serves: 8
Time: 25 minutes (+ 25-30 minute cool time)

Seeds are one of the healthiest snacks, but by themselves, they can be pretty bland. Kick things up a notch with these spicy jalapeno pumpkin seeds.

Ingredients:
3 sliced jalapeno peppers
1 ½ cups cleaned and dried pumpkin seeds
3 tablespoons olive oil
Sea salt to taste
Paprika to taste

Directions:
1. Preheat your oven to 350-degrees and spread the pumpkin seeds on a rimmed baking sheet.
2. Pour over the olive oil and salt generously.
3. Mix with your hands.
4. Put the sliced jalapeno on top, followed by the paprika.
5. Bake for 10 minutes.
6. When 10 minutes is up, stir and then bake for an additional 5 minutes.

7. Stir again, and bake again for another 5 minutes.
8. When time is up, let the seeds rest out of the oven for 15-30 minutes before eating.

<u>Nutritional info (⅛ recipe per serving)</u>
Calories: 189
Protein: 8
Carbs: 1
Fat: 17
Fiber: 2

Homemade Beef Jerky
Serves: 8
Time: 2 days, 5 hours

For this recipe, you'll need a dehydrator. You can make jerky in an oven, but it isn't quite the same. Making jerky takes a few days, but it's well-worth it to avoid all the preservatives and artificial ingredients in store-bought jerky.

<u>Ingredients:</u>
2 pounds trimmed rib eye
3 tablespoons coconut aminos
A pineapple core and rinds
A piece of ginger peel
Some cilantro stems
Honey to taste
Water

<u>Directions:</u>
1. In a pot, add all the ingredients except the meat and coconut aminos.
2. Add enough water to cover the marinade ingredients.
3. Boil until reduced by half, then remove from the heat.
4. Strain and cool.
5. While the sauce is boiling, prepare the steak by cutting it very thin, against the grain.
6. When the marinade is cooled, add the meat and marinade to a plastic bag and keep in the fridge for 1-2 days.
7. Bake in a dehydrator for 5 hours on 165-degrees.
8. The jerky should be hard and chewy.
9. Store in the fridge for up to a month.

Calories: 218
Protein: 25
Carbs: 1
Fat: 18
Fiber: 0

Cauliflower Popcorn
Serves: 4
Time: 1 hour

Regular popcorn isn't *bad* for you, but it isn't good either. It's basically empty calories. Cauliflower popcorn, however, is full of nutrients, and can be seasoned in a variety of ways. Here's a basic recipe to start with.

Ingredients:
1 head of cauliflower
4 tablespoons olive oil
Sea salt to taste

Directions:
1.   Preheat the oven to 425-degrees.
2.   Trim the cauliflower into florets.
3.   Cut the florets into ping pong-shaped pieces.
4.   In a bowl, combine the salt and olive oil, then toss the cauliflower in it.
5.   Line a baking sheet with parchment paper.
6.   Arrange the cauliflower on the sheet and bake for 1 hour, turning a few times.
7.   Serve right away!

Cooking Tip:

The browner the cauliflower, the sweeter they'll taste!

Nutritional info (¼ recipe per serving)
Calories: 145
Protein: 3
Carbs: 6
Fat: 14
Fiber: 2.9

Homemade Graham Crackers

Serves: 6
Time: 50 minutes

You probably ate a lot of graham crackers when you were a kid. As an adult, you probably don't eat them as much, except with s'mores, but they are great vehicles for nut butter. These homemade versions are grain-free, and use almond flour, chia seeds, and a little coconut flour.

Ingredients:
2 cups almond flour
¼ cup chia seeds
7 tablespoons hot water
¼ cup honey
2 tablespoons (+ 2 teaspoons) melted coconut oil
1 tablespoon ground cinnamon
2 teaspoons coconut flour
¼ teaspoon sea salt

Directions:
1. In a bowl, add the chia and hot water and stir.
2. Let that rest for 15 minutes to gel.
3. Preheat the oven to 300-degrees and prepare a pan with parchment paper.
4. Add the coconut oil and almond flour into the chia seed bowl.
5. In another bowl, combine the cinnamon, coconut flour, salt, and honey.
6. Scrape into the first bowl and stir.
7. Form the batter into a flat layer on the parchment paper pan.
8. Cut the shape of the crackers with a pizza cutter and poke each one with a fork a few times. The number of crackers depends on how many people you intend to serve.
9. Bake for 30-45 minutes, or until the crackers are hard.
10. Cool before eating.

Nutritional info (⅙ recipe per serving)
Calories: 344
Protein: 10
Carbs: 24
Fat: 27

Fiber: 2

Strawberry-Pineapple Ice Pops
Serves: 4
Time: 6 hours

Ice pops are a great summer treat, especially when you make your own. After a few minutes of prep, just wait for the pops to freeze, and you have a creamy, fruity snack that's so much better than anything you'd buy in a box.

Ingredients:
1 ½ cups fresh diced pineapple
1 cup full-fat coconut milk
1 cup fresh strawberries
1 ripe banana
1 tablespoon honey

Directions:
1. Puree the strawberries in a blender and move to a measuring cup.
2. Rinse out the blender.
3. Next, puree the pineapple, coconut milk, honey, and banana.
4. Pour a little of the strawberry puree into your Popsicle molds.
5. Pour in the pineapple puree ⅔ of the way, leaving a little room at the top.
6. Top off with more strawberry puree.
7. Freeze for 4-6 hours until solid.

Nutritional info (1 pop per serving)
Calories: 251
Protein: 3
Carbs: 41
Fat: 11
Fiber: 1.5

(Vegan) Chocolate-Cherry "Nice" Cream
Makes: 3 half-cup servings
Time: 3 hours, 15 minutes

"Nice" cream is one of my favorite treats. It's ice cream made from frozen bananas, and then customized with different fruits and flavors! Now, I know some of you might be side-eyeing this recipe because it uses chocolate, but it's 70%, organic dark chocolate, which is ok in my book.

Ingredients:
2 cups fresh cherries (or organic frozen if you can't find good fresh cherries)
½ banana
½ cup unsweetened almond milk
3 tablespoons chopped, 70% organic dark chocolate slivers

Directions:
1. Wash the cherries and remove their pits.
2. Put them in a Ziploc bag and stick in the freezer for at least 3 hours.
3. Put half of a peeled banana in the freezer. You can use the same bag as the cherries.
4. When you're ready to make the nice cream or at least 3 hours have passed, put the cherries, banana, and almond milk into a food processor and run.

Cooking Tip:

Put the ingredients in the freezer the night before you plan on making this dessert, and then it only takes 10 minutes!

5. Stir in the chocolate.
6. If the texture isn't as hard as you would like, stick in the freezer for another 5-10 minutes.

Nutritional info (½ cup per serving):
Calories: 126
Protein: 2.1
Carbs: 22.3
Fat: 4.0
Fiber: 2.8

Honey-Mango Fruit Leather
Serves: 4
Time: 10 hours

Fruit roll-ups are marketed to kids as a "healthy" snack, but they are packed with sugar and artificial flavors and colors. It isn't hard to make your own fruit leather, and you can experiment with flavor combinations for unique tastes. Here's one for mango.

Ingredients:
6 cups fresh, cubed mangos
½ cup honey
2 tablespoons lemon juice

Directions:
1. Put everything in a blender and process until smooth.
2. Line 2 cookie sheets with parchment paper and pour out the puree.
3. Bake in a 170-degree oven for 10 hours, or run in a dehydrator at 135-degrees for 8-10 hours.
4. When they are "tacky," they are done.
5. Cut out the size strips you want.

Nutritional info (¼ recipe per serving):
Calories: 271
Protein: 2
Carbs: 71
Fat: 1
Fiber: 3.9

Chapter 13 - Not-Skimpy Salads

Mason-Jar Taco Salads
Serves: 2
Time: 30 minutes

Salads in mason jars are extremely portable, and this one is also extremely tasty. It's packed with a variety of ingredients, including chicken, so you'll feel like you just had a loaded taco, but without the calorie-packed or messy tortilla.

Ingredients:
8-ounces of chicken breast cut into bite-sized pieces
Fresh spinach
2 chopped Roma tomatoes
1 cup sliced carrots
1 cup chopped cucumber
1 cup salsa
1 sliced red bell pepper
1 avocado
½ cup chopped onion
½ cup chopped cilantro
1 juiced lime
1 tablespoon olive oil
2 teaspoons cumin seed
2 teaspoons minced garlic

Directions:
1. Set out two wide-mouth quart mason jars.
2. Heat ½ tablespoon of olive oil and cook the chicken breast.
3. Set aside.
4. Add the rest of the oil to the pan and cook the carrots for about 3 minutes.
5. Turn the heat down to medium and add the garlic, pepper, and onion.
6. Continue cooking until they have softened and have charred edges.
7. In a separate pan, toast the cumin seeds for 2 minutes until golden brown.

8. Remove from the pan and crush them with the bottom of a glass.
9. Add the crushed seeds to the veggie pan.
10. Salt well and mix.
11. Mash the avocado and squirt with lime juice.
12. To make the salad, put ½ cup of salsa in the bottom of the jar.
13. Divide up the avocado and put on top of the salsa.
14. Do the same with the veggies and chicken.
15. Finish off with chopped tomatoes, cucumbers, and as much spinach as you can fit.
16. Seal the jar and store in the fridge until ready to eat.

Nutritional info (1 Mason jar salad per serving):
Calories: 529
Protein: 37
Carbs: 44
Fat: 29
Fiber: 7

Chicken-Almond Salad
Serves: 4
Time: 15 minutes

This chicken salad is bursting with grapes, blueberries, and almonds for a delicious variety of textures and flavors. The dressing is unique, too, and uses almond butter, so it provides protein in addition to taste.

Ingredients:
8-ounces cut chicken breasts
3 cups mixed greens
2 cups grapes
1 cup fresh blueberries
½ cup chopped almonds
1 teaspoon chili powder
Olive oil for cooking
Sea salt and black pepper
3 tablespoons water
3 tablespoons almond butter
2 tablespoons orange juice
1 tablespoon stone-ground mustard
1 tablespoon olive oil

½ tablespoon honey
½ minced garlic clove

Directions:
1. Season the chicken with chili powder, salt, and pepper.
2. Heat the olive oil in a skillet on medium-high.
3. Cook the chicken until done - about 8 to 10 minutes.
4. Plate the chicken and shred when cool to touch.
5. Combine all the ingredients in the second ingredient list and stir well.
6. In a bowl, add the greens, grapes, almonds, blueberries, and chicken.
7. Pour the dressing on top and enjoy!

Nutritional info (¼ recipe per serving):
Calories: 353
Protein: 21
Carbs: 23
Fat: 22
Fiber: 1

Chipotle Sweet Potato Salad
Serves: 4
Time: 45 minutes

Rich, nutty sweet potatoes are roasted with some coconut oil, and then tossed in a salad with avocado, red onion, and cherry tomatoes. A creamy, spicy chipotle dressing ties everything together, and balances out the sweetness of the potato and acid of the onion and tomatoes.

Ingredients:
4 medium-sized, diced sweet potatoes
½ cup homemade mayo
½ cup cherry tomatoes
1 diced avocado
1 diced red onion
2 tablespoons melted coconut oil
1 tablespoon apple cider vinegar
1 tablespoon chipotle peppers in adobo sauce
1 tablespoon fresh lime juice
½ teaspoon cumin powder
Sea salt and black pepper to taste

Directions:
1. Preheat the oven to 375-degrees.
2. Mix the diced sweet potatoes with the melted coconut oil.
3. Arrange on a baking pan and bake for 30 minutes.
4. In a separate bowl, mix the mayo, cumin, vinegar, lime juice, and chipotle sauce, and season with pepper and salt.
5. Add the sweet potato pieces, onion, avocado, and cherry tomatoes, and stir.
6. Chill in the fridge for an hour or eat right away.

Nutritional info (¼ recipe per serving):
Calories: 439
Protein: 22
Carbs: 28
Fat: 51
Fiber: 7

Bacon-Fennel Salad w/ Grilled Peaches
Serves: 4-6
Time: About 25 minutes

Fennel is not only extremely good for you, it's aromatic and a little bit sweet, which is perfect for this salad with ripe peaches and bacon. When you cook the bacon, be sure to keep 2 tablespoons of fat for the dressing.

Ingredients:
3-4 ripe peaches
1 cup of chopped fennel bulb
4 pieces of chopped, cooked bacon
2 tablespoons coconut oil
Mixed salad greens
Sea salt to taste
5 tablespoons olive oil
4 pitted dates
2 tablespoons apple cider vinegar
2 tablespoons bacon fat
1 slice of cooked bacon

Directions:
1. Begin by grilling the peaches.
2. Cut them in half and remove the pit.

3. Brush with melted cocon
4. Place them cut-side dow
   the lid.
5. Grill for 12-14 minutes, cl
6. While those grill, melt cod
7. Sauté the fennel for 4-5 m
8. Cool.
9. To make the dressing,
   ingredient list until smoot
10. To make the salads, mix
    with the fennel and chopp
11. Add the grilled peaches on

1 teaspoon homemade my

Directions:
1. Mix the
2. everyth
3. Make
4. ca

Nutritional info (¼ recipe per serving):
Calories: 470
Protein: 10
Carbs: 20
Fat: 40
Fiber: 4

Spicy Scallop Salad
Serves: 4
Time: About 10 minutes

This green salad for four only takes ten minutes, but comes with a lot of great ingredients, including bay scallops seasoned with cayenne pepper. A 3-ounce scallop contains a whopping 17 grams of protein and only 95 calories, making them a very nutrient dense food.

Ingredients:
1 pound bay scallops
2 handfuls of greens
½ cup olive oil
1 seeded red bell pepper cut into strips
1 cubed avocado
1 minced garlic clove
3 tablespoons coconut oil
3 tablespoons lemon juice
1 tablespoon homemade mayo
2 teaspoons black pepper
2 teaspoons cayenne pepper
1 teaspoon sea salt

stard

greens, peppers, and avocado in a bowl, so
ing will be ready once the scallops are cooked.
e the vinaigrette by mixing the mayo, lemon juice,
yenne, mustard, salt, and pepper.
Slowly add in the olive oil.
In another bowl, mix the cayenne and a little more salt and
pepper.

5. Rinse the scallops and pat dry.
6. Coat the scallops in the cayenne seasoning mix
7. Heat a skillet over medium and melt the coconut oil.
8. When it's hot enough to sear the scallops, cook the scallops
   for 2 minutes on each side until opaque.
9. Plate the scallops on top of the mixed greens and pour over
   the dressing.
10. Serve right away!

Nutritional info (¼ recipe per serving):
Calories: 577
Protein: 27
Carbs: 13
Fat: 52
Fiber: 4

Rainbow Shrimp Salad
Serves: 4
Time: 15 minutes

Taste the rainbow with this colorful and high-protein salad. There's
green from the arugula, red from the cabbage, orange from the
carrot, and gold from the mango. Everything gets mixed together
with a simple lime juice-based dressing and topped with grilled
shrimp. Yum!

Ingredients:
Two big handfuls of arugula
20 large shrimp
¼ head of red cabbage
2 chopped green onions
2 large carrots
1 mango

1 bunch of cilantro
A handful of cashews
¼ cup lime juice
3 tablespoons Red Boat fish sauce
2 tablespoons honey
Red pepper flakes to taste

Directions:
1. Julienne the carrots, mango, and red cabbage.
2. Chop up the cilantro and green onion.
3. Preheat the oven to 350-degrees and toast the cashews for 6-10 minutes.
4. Season the shrimp with salt and pepper, and grill for 2 minutes on each side.
5. Mix the arugula, veggies, mango, cashews, green onions, and cilantro together.
6. Top with grilled shrimp.
7. To make the dressing, whisk the honey, lime juice, fish sauce, and red pepper flakes together until the honey dissolves.
8. Pour the dressing over the salad and serve.

Nutritional info (¼ recipe per serving):
Calories: 292
Protein: 38
Carbs: 28
Fat: 8
Fiber: 4

Avocado-Tuna Salad
Serves: 1
Time: Less than 5 minutes

Skip the plates when you choose this tuna salad. You use the hollowed-out shells of an avocado, and stuff it with a mixture of the avocado flesh, cooked tuna, and chopped onion. It's extremely filling and high in fiber.

Ingredients:
5 ounces of cooked tuna
1 avocado
1 juiced lemon
1 tablespoon chopped onion

Sea salt and black pepper to taste

Directions:
1. Cut the avocado in half.
2. Remove the pit and most of the avocado flesh.
3. Put the avocado flesh in a bowl.
4. Add the lemon juice and onion, and mash together.
5. Put in the tuna, season with salt and pepper, and mix.
6. Scoop the salad into the avocado skins and enjoy!

Nutritional info (1 recipe per serving):
Calories: 547
Protein: 47
Carbs: 26
Fat: 31
Fiber: 13

Beet, Blood Orange, + Fennel Salad
Serve: 4-6

Traditionally from Morocco, this salad is one of the most beautiful and healthy salads you could make. You use two colors of beets - red and gold - as well as navel and blood oranges. The flavors are out of this world, as is the nutrition.

Ingredients:
3 blood oranges
2 medium-sized golden beets, with tops trimmed
2 medium-sized red beets, with tops trimmed
¼ cup loosely-packed cilantro
1 medium-sized navel orange
1 tablespoon fresh lime juice
1 tablespoon fresh lemon juice
½ fennel bulb, sliced very thin with a mandolin
⅓ cup very thinly-sliced red onion
Olive oil
Sea salt and black pepper to taste

Directions:
1. Preheat the oven to 400-degrees.
2. Wash the beets.
3. Wrap each beet individually in foil and roast on a rimmed baking sheet for 1 hour.

4. Peel the oranges, getting rid of the white part.
5. Cut between 2 blood oranges' membranes to get the segments, and squeeze the membranes for their juice into the bowl, too.
6. Slice up the rest of the blood oranges, and cut the navel orange into thin rounds.
7. Add the citrus juices.
8. Once the beets are done, peel and cut two of them into thin rounds.
9. Cut the rest into wedges.
10. Plate the beets and oranges.
11. Add the fennel and onion.
12. Drizzle everything with a good-quality olive oil, and season with sea salt and pepper.
13. Let the salad rest for 5 minutes or so before garnishing with cilantro and serving.

Nutritional info (¼ recipe per serving):
Calories: 111
Protein: 3
Carbs: 25
Fat: 0
Fiber: 6

Salmon Veggie Bowl

Serves: 1
Time: 15 minutes

For a great way to use up leftover salmon, look to this salad. It uses 4 ounces of salmon tossed with some mixed greens, and dressed up with sautéed zucchini and fresh raspberries.

Ingredients:
3 cups mixed greens
4-ounces of baked salmon
½ cup raspberries
½ cup sliced zucchini
2 tablespoons olive oil
1 tablespoon balsamic vinegar
A sprig of thyme
Lemon juice
Sea salt and pepper to taste

Directions:
1. Heat ½ tablespoon of olive oil in a skillet and sauté the zucchini for 5 minutes.
2. If you aren't using leftover salmon, bake the uncooked salmon for 10 minutes at 400-degrees with 1 tablespoon of olive oil, salt, pepper, and lemon juice.
3. To build the salad, add a generous helping of greens to a bowl, followed by the zucchini, then salmon.
4. Drizzle over a little olive oil and balsamic vinegar.
5. Toss everything together before finishing off with the thyme and raspberries.

Nutritional info (1 recipe per serving):
Calories: 421
Protein: 15
Carbs: 14
Fat: 34
Fiber: 5

Grapefruit-Lobster Salad
Serves: 2
Time: 15 minutes

Lots of people don't really think of a salad as being "gourmet," but this one definitely is. A pound of pre-cooked lobster is dressed in olive oil, grapefruit juice, chives, and white-wine vinegar, before being mixed with greens, slices of avocado, and grapefruit pieces.

Ingredients:
1 pound of pre-cooked lobster
2-3 cups of mixed greens
1 pitted and sliced avocado
1 segmented and peeled grapefruit
4 tablespoons olive oil
2 tablespoons white-wine vinegar
1 tablespoon minced chives
1 minced shallot
2 teaspoons fresh grapefruit juice
Fresh dill
Sea salt and pepper to taste

Directions:

1. To make the dressing, whisk the vinegar, olive oil, shallot, chives, grapefruit juice, and salt and pepper together.
2. Toss the lobster with the dressing.
3. In a separate bowl, add the greens, grapefruit, and avocado.
4. Add the lobster and fresh dill to the bowl, and drizzle on any remaining dressing.

Nutritional info (½ recipe per serving):
Calories: 564
Protein: 30
Carbs: 35
Fat: 39
Fiber: 9

Epilogue

After reading this book, I hope you feel prepared to take out processed foods and make the switch to whole foods. I also hope you are excited to try out any of the awesome 120 recipes! They will prove to you that living clean and whole in today's world is possible - it just takes a little more focus and planning. Your health is worth it, though.

When you eat whole, you will be supplying your body with the vital nutrients that processed foods strip out, like Vitamin D, Vitamin B12, fiber, iron, and more. You will have more energy, become ill less often, and strengthen your body against terminal illnesses, like cancer and Alzheimer's. If you have struggled to manage your weight in the past, eating whole-foods can help with that, too, though this book is not written as a "diet," per say. The ultimate goal is to cleanse your system from harmful artificial ingredients and chemicals, and instead supply it with the nutrients it needs to thrive. If weight loss is a result of that process, that's great!

When you start eating whole foods and changing your lifestyle, you will hit some rough patches, but don't worry. Set up a system where you give yourself grace when you trip up and find support in your friends and family. It's impossible to be perfect all the time, and the longer you eat whole foods, the easier it will become to avoid the processed and packaged stuff. Good luck and happy (whole) eating!

Thank you for reading this book!

I hope the book was able to teach you how whole foods can dramatically improve your health and well-being.

Finally, if you enjoyed this book, then I'd like to ask you for a favor, would you be kind enough to leave a review for this book on Amazon? It'd be greatly appreciated!

Preview of Ketogenic Diet Cookbook: 80 Easy, Delicious, and Healthy Recipes to Help You Lose Weight, Boost Your Energy, and Prevent Cancer, Stroke and Alzheimer`s

The kitchen is where the majority of my most treasured memories have taken place. From the time my mother used to drag out the stool so I could cut cookies and stir sauces on the countertop up until now, there is no place which makes me feel more at home. And the ketogenic diet has only added to my most wonderful cooking experiences!

This is the largest compilation of recipes I have ever put into one book, and I can't tell you how excited I am to be able to share it with you! The thought of you digging into a home cooked meal which was tried and tested in my kitchen first truly warms my heart. Not only that, but to think that you will benefit health-wise as well really makes me feel proud about what I'm doing. As my mother used to say, "Food brings people together, but good food brings people closer together."

And that's just what my cookbook is all about – *good food!* While it's true that the ketogenic diet can be bland, as any diet can, using the right ingredients means creating dishes you'll be craving as soon as the day after. Almost every recipe in this book uses indulgent amounts of coconut oil, butter, heavy cream, bacon, and my favorite – CHEESE! You're sure to find something for every mood of every day. From classic comfort foods to mouth-watering veggie-rich dishes, this book really has it all.

As the title of this book reads, the ketogenic diet can result in some pretty amazing health benefits, all of which I will go over in following chapters. With obesity rates climbing and disease on the rise, I'm proud to bring to you an assortment of savory dishes which both your taste buds and your body will thank you for. What can I say? My life revolves around this stuff... it's what I do.

So, let's bring that kitchen of yours back to life! Feel free to experiment with spices and double or triple recipes when you're expecting guests. And hey, if a recipe doesn't come out right the first time, take a breather, remember you're human, and try again.

Although most of these recipes are extremely easy to follow, practice still does make perfect! There's no doubt in my mind that you'll become quite the keto-expert in no time.

MY OTHER BOOKS

Ketogenic Diet - Achieve Rapid Weight Loss while Gaining Incredible Health and Energy

Ketogenic Diet-2 in 1 Box Set-A Complete Guide to the Ketogenic Diet-115 Amazing Recipes for Weight Loss and Improved Health

Mediterranean Diet for Beginners-50 Amazing Recipes for Weight Loss and Improved Health

Mediterranean Diet Cookbook: 105 Easy, Irresistible, and Healthy Recipes for Weight Loss and Improved Quality of Life While Minimizing the Risk of Disease

Mediterranean Diet-2 in 1 Box Set: A Comprehensive Guide to the Mediterranean Diet-155 Mouth-Watering and Healthy Recipes to Help You Lose Weight, Increase Your Energy Level and Prevent Disease

Pressure Cooker Cookbook: 100 Quick, Easy, and Healthy Pressure Cooker Recipes for Nourishing and Delicious Meals

Pressure Cooker Cookbook-110 Quick, Easy, and Delicious Pressure Cooker Recipes for Electric and Stove Top Pressure Cookers

Electric Pressure Cooker Cookbook: 60 Quick, Easy, and Healthy Pressure Cooker Recipes for Electric Pressure Cookers

Electric Pressure Cooker Cookbook- 100 Quick, Easy, and Healthy Recipes for Electric Pressure Cookers

Pressure Cooker Cookbook-2 in 1 Box Set-200 Mouth-Watering and Healthy Pressure Cooker Recipes for Stove Top and Electric Pressure Cookers

Pressure Cooker Cookbook-3 in 1 Box Set-310 Mouth-Watering and Healthy Pressure Cooker Recipes for Stove Top and Electric Pressure Cookers

Pressure Cooker Cookbook-4 in 1 Box Set-370 Quick, Easy, and Healthy Pressure Cooker Recipes for Amazingly Tasty and Nourishing Meals

I would love to give you a bonus. Please visit happyhealthycookingonline.com and get these 4 amazing eBooks for FREE!

Made in the USA
Lexington, KY
25 April 2017